Khristina,

OVER
COME

Get off the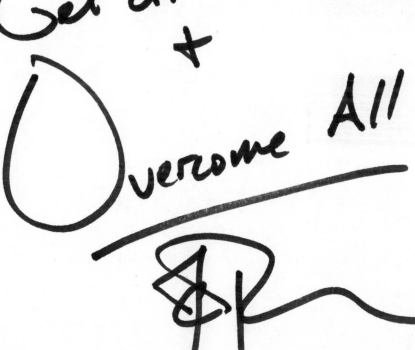
+
Overcome All

OVER
COME

CRUSH ADVERSITY WITH THE LEADERSHIP
TECHNIQUES OF AMERICA'S TOUGHEST WARRIORS

JASON REDMAN

CENTER
STREET

New York Nashville

Center Street
Hachette Book Group
1290 Avenue of the Americas, New York, NY 10104
centerstreet.com
twitter.com/centerstreet

First Edition: December 2019

Center Street is a division of Hachette Book Group, Inc. The Center Street name and logo are trademarks of Hachette Book Group, Inc.

The publisher is not responsible for websites (or their content) that are not owned by the publisher.

The Hachette Speakers Bureau provides a wide range of authors for speaking events. To find out more, go to www.HachetteSpeakersBureau.com or call (866) 376-6591.

LCCN: 2019951937

ISBNs: 978-1-5460-8471-6 (hardcover), 978-1-5460-8470-9 (ebook)

Printed in the United States of America

LSC-C

Printing 5, 2022

This book is dedicated to my Long-Haired Admiral.
Your love, leadership, and wise counsel have helped guide me through my major life ambushes.
You have been my light in the darkness.

This book is also dedicated to my Naval Special Warfare brothers.
Those still here who helped forge my leadership and Overcome Mind-Set.
And those who answered the call after 9/11 and never made it back home.

Ensign (SEAL) Jerry "Buck" Pope—Yemen—2002
HMC (SEAL) Matthew J. Bourgeois—Afghanistan—2002
ABH1 (SEAL) Neil C. Roberts—Afghanistan—2002
CDR (SEAL) Peter G. Oswald, El Salvador—2002
PH1 (SEAL) David M. Tapper—Afghanistan—2003
IT2 (SEAL) Mario Maestas—Training—2003
IC1 (SEAL) Thomas E. Retzer—Afghanistan—2003
BM1 (SEAL) Brian Ouellette—Afghanistan—2004
BM1 (SWCC) Robert P. Vetter—Training—2004
BMCS (SEAL) Theodore D. Fitzhenry—Training—2004
LT (SEAL) Michael P. Murphy—Afghanistan—2005
GM2 (SEAL) Danny P. Dietz—Afghanistan—2005
STG2 (SEAL) Matthew G. Axelson—Afghanistan—2005
ITCS (SEAL) Daniel R. Healy—Afghanistan—2005
QM2 (SEAL) James Suh—Afghanistan—2005
MM2 (SEAL) Shane Patton—Afghanistan—2005
LCDR (SEAL) Erik S. Kristensen—Afghanistan—2005
LT (SEAL) Michael M. McGreevy Jr.—Afghanistan—2005
FCC (SEAL) Jacques J. Fontan—Afghanistan—2005
ET1 (SEAL) Jeffrey S. Taylor—Afghanistan—2005
ET1 (SEAL) Jeffrey A. Lucas—Afghanistan—2005
AO2 (SEAL) Marc A. Lee—Iraq—2006
MA2 (SEAL) Michael A. Monsoor—Iraq—2006
SN Freddie Porter—Training—2007
SO2 Joseph C. Schwedler—Iraq—2007
SO1 Jason D. Lewis—Iraq—2007
MC1 Robert R. McRill—Iraq—2007
CTT1 Steven P. Daugherty—Iraq—2007
SOC Mark T. Carter—Iraq—2007
SOC Jason R. Freiwald—Afghanistan—2008
SOCS John W. Marcum—Afghanistan—2008
SO1 Joshua T. Harris—Afghanistan—2008
SOCS Thomas J. Valentine—Training—2008
SOC Lance M. Vaccaro—Training—2008

SO2 Shapoor "Alex" Ghane—Training—2008
EOD1 Louis Soufront—Iraq—2008
SOC Michael Koch—Iraq—2008
SOC Nathan Hardy—Iraq—2008
PR1 Andrew J. Lightner—Training—2009
SOC Eric F. Shellenberger—Training—2009
SO2 Ryan Job—Wounded Iraq 2006—United States—2009
EOD2 Tyler J. Trahan—Iraq—2009
LT Brendan J. Looney—Afghanistan—2010
CTRCS David B. McClendon—Afghanistan—2010
SO2 Adam O. Smith—Afghanistan—2010
SO3 Dennis C. Miranda—Afghanistan—2010
SOC Adam Brown—Afghanistan—2010
SO1 Tyler Stimson—United States—2010
SO2 Ronald Woodle—Training—2010
SOC Collin Thomas—Afghanistan—2010
SO1 Caleb A. Nelson—Afghanistan—2011
LCDR (SEAL) Jonas Kelsall—Afghanistan—2011
SOCM Louis Langlais—Afghanistan—2011
SOCS Thomas Ratzlaff—Afghanistan—2011
SOCS Robert Reeves—Afghanistan—2011
SOCS Heath Robinson—Afghanistan—2011
EODCS Kraig Vickers—Afghanistan—2011
SOC Brian Bill—Afghanistan—2011
SO1 Aaron Vaughn—Afghanistan—2011
SO1 Christopher Campbell—Afghanistan—2011
SO1 Darrik Benson—Afghanistan—2011
IT1 Jared Day—Afghanistan—2011
SO1 Jason Workman—Afghanistan—2011
SO1 Jesse Pittman—Afghanistan—2011
MA1 John Douangdara—Afghanistan—2011
SOC John Faas—Afghanistan—2011
SO1 John Tumilson—Afghanistan—2011
SOC Kevin Houston—Afghanistan—2011
SOC Matthew Mason—Afghanistan—2011

CTR1 Michael Strange—Afghanistan—2011
EODC Nicholas Null—Afghanistan—2011
SO2 Nicholas Spehar—Afghanistan—2011
SOC Stephen Mills—Afghanistan—2011
LT Thomas C. Fouke—Training—2012
SO1 Patrick D. Feeks—Afghanistan—2012
SO1 David J. Warsen—Afghanistan—2012
GM2 Dion R. Roberts—Afghanistan—2012
SO1 Matthew G. Kantor—Afghanistan—2012
SO1 Kevin R. Ebbert—Afghanistan—2012
SO1 Nicolas D. Checque—Afghanistan—2012
CDR (SEAL) Job Price—Afghanistan—2012
SO1 Matthew Leathers—Training—2013
CTT Christian M. Pike—Afghanistan—2013
SOC Chris Kyle—United States—2013
SOC Brett Shadle—Training—2013
SO3 Jonathan H. Kaloust—Training—2013
SOC Brad Cavner—Training—2014
SO1 William Marston—Training—2015
SO3 Jason Kortz—Training—2015
SOCM Bryan Beiriger—United States—2015
Seaman James Lovelace—Training—2016
SOC Charles Keating—Iraq—2016
EODC Jason Finan—Iraq—2016
SO1 Devon J. Grube—United States—2016
SOCS William "Ryan" Owens—Yemen—2017
SOCS Kyle Milliken—Somalia—2017
SO1 Remington Peters—Training—2017
LT (SEAL) Mark Weiss—Tanzania—2017
SOC Eduardo Valadez—United States—2017
CDR (SEAL) Seth Stone—United States—2017
SO3 Justin Pegg—United States—2018
SOCS Chad Michael Wilkinson—United States—2018
LTJG (SEAL) David Metcalf—United States—2019

Your sacrifice continues to inspire me to never take a day for granted and to wake
up every day to get off the X and Overcome.

CONTENTS

CONTENTS

INTRODUCTION

WHAT IS A LIFE AMBUSH?

IN SEPTEMBER 2007, I AWOKE GROGGY IN BETHESDA NAVAL HOSPITAL with tubes running from every opening in my body, the heart monitor beeping. The previous week had been a total blur, with vast periods of time completely lost. I remembered waking up in the Combat Support Hospital in Baghdad, where I'd been med-evaced after my team was caught in an ambush. I remembered waking up in Balad, Iraq, where they take soldiers with combat head wounds for treatment. Time vanished, and then I woke up in Landstuhl, Germany, for more emergency surgeries and blood transfusions. I remember the chaotic flight home where multiple times I thought I was going to suffocate due to excessive congestion in my tracheotomy. And I remember the surreal feeling of being back on American soil, riding in the blue bus to Bethesda Naval Hospital.

Now I was lying in my hospital bed, weak and barely able to move, as a young, energetic doctor talked me through the path ahead. Despite everything, I was determined to get out of the hospital as fast as possible. But I couldn't say that to the doctor, due to my extensive facial wounds and the tracheotomy. I couldn't move my left arm after it was nearly sheared off by enemy gunfire. The only way I could communicate was through writing.

"Doc, how many months will it take to put me back together," I wrote on the pad on my lap, "so I can get back to the fight and my teammates?"

Her face registered disbelief. She shook her head.

"Months?" she said. "Lieutenant, we're talking years to put you back together."

I sank back into my bed. Years.

When I had been selected for the Seaman to Admiral program and spent three years at Old Dominion University to get my degree, I had missed years of experience with my teammates. I wasn't going to miss years alongside them again if I had anything to do with it. I'd had moments of disbelief, grief, fear, and pain as I lay there in the hospital taking one day at a time, but thinking about my teammates fighting in Iraq without me had kept me determined to get back to combat as soon as possible. I knew I could defy the odds like I had so many times before.

A few days later, two visitors came in and began to talk about what bad shape I was in.

"What a shame," they said, as I drifted in and out of sleep. "What a shame we send these young men and women off to war and they come home broken. They will never be the same. Most will struggle to make it back into society. Most will never be whole. What a waste."

I couldn't talk, and although I still had some ringing in my ears from the bullet that had torn half my face off, I could hear just fine. As I listened to them talk about me, I felt something stirring in my gut.

For my entire life, I had beaten the odds. I made it into the SEALs, the most elite fighting force in the world, despite being a small, skinny high schooler with discipline problems and unimpressive grades. After almost being washed out of the Navy because of a leadership failure early in my career as an officer, I had fought my way back to being a respected officer and leader and was ready to assume the first major level of SEAL command, platoon commander. I was at the height of my career.

But all of that was before I had run into the devastating ambush that had wounded me and two of my teammates and left my blood and pieces of my body on the battlefield in Iraq. Were these people, these supposed friends, right? Was this how things were going to be now? Was this how people were going to see me? A cripple, a disfigured man forever ruined by a war that had claimed so many, a powerless victim?

Was I going to be looked down on for the rest of my life as an object of pity?

These questions rattled through my mind, and I broke into a cold sweat as I replayed the events of the night only a week before when everything changed.

That night, my US Navy SEAL task unit had received last-minute intel on the location of a time-sensitive target in the Al Karmah area of Al Anbar Province in Iraq. A senior-level Al Qaeda commander had been reported in a compound in our area of responsibility. He was a dangerous individual we had been tracking all deployment. Once our mission was cleared, I began preparing, triple-checking my gear, running over the battle plan in my head until I knew it inside and out. Then, my team and I boarded the Black Hawk helicopters that would drop us into battle.

When my team landed, we easily took over the compound, encountering no resistance. In the main building, we uncovered a weapons cache and jihadist propaganda, but either the intel was incorrect or something had alerted the enemy that we were coming, because our target was nowhere to be found.

Our snipers on the rooftop suddenly began notifying us of activity nearby.

"Red, there's movement outside . . ."

We soon discovered that our enemy was in a house roughly 150 yards from the one we had cleared. We pushed an Air Force AC-130 gunship overhead. The gunship reported that men were in motion from the other house, so I took my assault team and patrolled in their direction. As we approached their position, my team got separated because of a radio frequency miscommunication.

We quickly maneuvered through a dense thicket to combine our forces, but as we struggled through the Iraqi chaparral, my team and I were caught in a deadly, well-executed ambush with the Al Qaeda commander's handpicked personal security detail. In the ensuing thirty-five-minute firefight, three of us were severely wounded.

I was shot the first time when a hidden machine-gun nest just ten yards from my position opened fire. I was hit immediately, bullets stitching across my midsection. Most embedded themselves in my body armor, but two rounds struck my left arm, nearly shearing it in half. In the confusion of the fight, I thought my arm had been severed from my body. Bullets continued to ricochet off my gun, my night-vision goggles, and my helmet as I struggled to understand the ambush and lead us out of it. There were two enemy machine guns firing from only fifty feet away, as well as a dozen enemy AK-47 shooters. I was stranded in a devastating cross fire of thousands of rounds the size of my thumb.

Fear and terror attempted to grip my mind, but I pushed them away. I knew I had to get to cover or I was going to die right there, on that spot. I looked behind me and saw nothing but thousands of yards of empty Iraqi desert. Then I saw muzzle flashes from my teammates shooting past me at the enemy. There was a large John Deere–style tractor tire my teammates had jumped behind to make their last stand against an overwhelming enemy force. Cover. Something that would stop bullets and give us a position to fight back from.

Despite my injuries and pain, hope welled in my soul. I had to get to that tire. I rose to run to the only cover available, but as I leapt forward, a bullet struck in front of my right ear and traveled through my face, blasting off my nose, blowing out my cheekbone, vaporizing my right orbital floor, and shattering all the bones above my eye. The guys at the tire saw my head whip-saw forward and watched me collapse and crash into the ground ten yards in front of them. I blacked out as my blood soaked into the foreign soil.

When I came to, I was caught in the open, on the X, the kill zone, the point of attack, while the firefight continued to rage over me. I was bleeding out, caught between my team and two machine guns that had nearly killed me. Anger that I had allowed us to get into this situation slowly gave way to the realization that I was going to die.

If you have studied the body and trauma long enough and witnessed others sustain grievous battlefield injuries, you recognize the error codes as they come. It's similar to a mechanic with a diagnostic computer coding a broken car. This amazing machine we walk around in operates off specific pressures, and if you spring a leak—due to large bullets tearing through your body, for instance—your pressures start to drop and the machine goes into emergency mode. Without enough blood volume to push to the entire body, it starts to pool blood into your most vital organs. When this happens, your extremities go numb and get cold, and your body goes into shock. This is what I was experiencing. I knew I was dying.

I could feel the life slipping out of me. To be honest, it was a luxury, knowing I was dying. For some people, death comes in a millisecond. They don't even realize it's coming. For me, I was lying in that firefight for thirty-five minutes, which left ample time to reflect.

Drifting in and out of consciousness, I could feel myself going through the different stages of shock. I started getting really cold. I couldn't feel my extremities anymore. I tried to move my right hand, which wasn't injured, but I couldn't move it. I felt like I couldn't breathe. Every draw of breath took more and more effort, and it got harder and harder to think.

In the moments when I could think, my family flooded my mind, along with the grim realization that I would never go home again. I would never hold my wife, raise my son to be a strong man, walk my daughters down the aisle, celebrate Christmas. It was a crushing reality.

I remember regretting my poor decisions as well as the opportunities I'd passed on, and more than anything, I wanted just a few more seconds to tell my family that I loved them.

I lay there dying, knowing one cold, hard fact of combat: my teammates could not rush out and save me. Warriors have learned the hard lessons of rushing into open gunfire to save fallen comrades and getting wounded or killed themselves. The rules of warfare are simple: kill or be killed. The rules of an ambush are simple: fight back and win, and don't put yourself in a position where you can't fight. We have been trained to win the firefight first and save our teammates second, because you cannot win and save them if you are wounded or dead. I lay there in this grim reality, knowing I had to be patient and trust my teammates. But I knew I had limited time. Every pump of my heart pushed more and more blood out of my body and sent me one additional step closer to the end.

As I struggled to focus and think through the fierce gunfire, I called out to God: "Lord, give me the strength."

Upon that prayer, a thought popped into my head. I had watched a documentary by Jon Alpert and Matthew O'Neill called *Baghdad ER* (2006), and I remembered a line from it: "Our military trauma doctors are so good that if you can show up at the Combat Support Hospital [CSH] with a pulse, you have a 90 percent chance of surviving."

I wrapped my head around this singular thought: *Stay awake to stay alive.* In the midst of the chaos, that became what I focused on. I said to myself, "I don't care what happens. If I have to reach into my own chest and pump my own heart with my bare fist, I'm going to arrive at that CSH alive."

With my team holding ground, the AC-130 finally released their first fire mission, and they took down the last of the enemy with precision fire. I had called in danger-close fire missions before, but this was closer than anything I'd ever seen. "Danger close" is a military term for the proximity to explosions and fragmentation from aerial munitions. Much smarter people than me had performed countless tests on every type of military bomb and bullet and measured the farthest distance the explosive shockwave and metal fragmentation traveled from the point of impact. These "danger rings" were called "danger-close" parameters, and as a leader on the ground we knew depending on the munitions being used how far we had to be from the enemy to be out of the danger zone. If you were inside of the danger zone, you were danger close or within the impact area. Pilots and flight crews tried to actively avoid dropping danger-close munitions because they knew the possibility of wounding or killing friendly forces was incredibly high the closer the danger-close mission was to your position. My team leader had to call fire directly on our position, literally only a few yards away from me, to push the enemy back. This was as danger close as it got. I watched the rounds impact the ground directly in front of us and explode, sending dirt, debris, and fragments directly over our heads. These fire missions ended up being the closest rounds dropped near friendly forces in the entire Iraq War, and they also saved our lives and enabled us to finally win the gunfight.

The medevac landed about seventy-five yards from my

position, and my team leader said it was time for me to go. The average human body has eight to twelve units of blood coursing through it. Later, when that helicopter arrived at the combat hospital, I would need four units of blood. But despite my severe blood loss, despite the fact that I had been completely unable to move minutes before, I somehow got up and hobbled to the helicopter under my own power. Later, when the docs at the Baghdad hospital heard this, they couldn't believe it. Considering the severity of my injuries, most people probably wouldn't have survived, let alone made it out under their own power.

Stay awake to stay alive. Overcome.

Back at the hospital in Bethesda, as the pity and stares of my guests bounced off the inside of my damaged brain, that was the moment I thought of.

I was lucky to be alive. I knew that. Shouldn't that be enough? the looks and whispers seemed to say. I began to doubt myself. Was a full recovery too much to hope for? Shouldn't I be content to just be breathing? Wasn't getting my hopes up for what seemed impossible—getting back to the man I had been—just setting myself up for a bigger fall later?

Maybe this was it. Maybe I needed to accept the fact that I would always be less than I had been.

But why did that feel so much like quitting? Why did it feel like giving in?

That stinging in my gut turned into a burning.

I thought back to my failure as a leader and hitting rock

bottom, and my journey back from failure to growth and from growth to redemption.

No, I had been in harder, deeper, darker pain and adversity than this.

The pity party left. My wife, Erica, the Long-Haired Admiral, returned to my room. I motioned for her to hand me my notepad. I began to write furiously, my one good hand racing across the page.

"Attention: to all who enter here," I wrote. "If you are coming into this room with sorrow or to feel sorry for my wounds, go elsewhere. The wounds I received, I got in a job I love, doing it for people I love, supporting the freedom of a country I deeply love. I am incredibly tough and will make a full recovery. What is full? That is the absolute utmost physically my body has the ability to recover. Then I will push that about 20 percent further through sheer mental tenacity. This room you are about to enter is a room of fun, optimism, and intense rapid regrowth. If you are not prepared for that, go elsewhere. From: the management."

I set down my pen, took a deep breath, and motioned for Erica to tape the note to the door.

Never again, I thought. Never again would I let anyone look at me with pity. Never again would I look at myself with pity. I would OVERCOME.

Since then I have undergone forty reconstructive surgeries. I have had six blood transfusions, and I wore a tracheostomy for seven months and two days. I've had approximately 1,500 stitches, two hundred staples, five plates, a titanium orbital floor, fifteen screws, eight pins, twenty skin grafts, and four bone grafts, including a calvarial bone graft. I have had my jaw shattered, broken, and rebroken three times. My mouth was wired shut for over twelve weeks. I lost over fifty pounds. I have spent approximately 190 hours in surgery under anesthesia. Despite all that, I'm still standing, I'm still breathing, and most of all, I am still in control of my destiny. In the immortal words of my favorite poem, "Invictus," *I am the master of my fate, I am the captain of my soul.*

As it happened, on the day I wrote and hung the sign on my hospital door, there was a legendary New York fire captain and marine named John Vigiano visiting. Vigiano had lost both sons on 9/11. To heal his broken soul and to motivate wounded warriors, Vigiano started making regular pilgrimages to Bethesda. That day, he saw my sign, took a picture of it, and posted it on social media.

Then something amazing happened. Within a few days, his post went viral. *CBS This Morning* and other major news programs talked about it. National newspapers wrote articles about it. President George W. Bush invited my family to the White House, and I got to shake his hand in the Oval Office and look him in the eye as he thanked me for my service to our great country. What came to be known as "The Sign on the Door" was seen by many people as a perfect illustration of the American spirit to persevere in the midst of challenges. For me, it was a message to the world that I was ready for the next challenge.

After the Sign on the Door went viral, I was approached about writing a book to share my SEAL career, my near-death experience, and my rebirth with the world. *The Trident: The Forging and Reforging of a Navy SEAL Leader* was a huge success and led to appearances on national television, speaking events all over the world, and thousands of conversations with wounded warriors and individuals seeking to recover from their own life ambushes—those traumatic, catastrophic incidents in our lives that threaten to kill us or keep us from truly living afterward.

One of the wounded warriors I met during one of these events was James. During a Q&A, he raised his hand and proceeded to tell me in a quiet voice that everything I had just spoken about might sound great, but none of it could fix his problem.

I might have brushed him off as an angry guy who just didn't get it, but that day I felt like I needed to hear James out. So I asked him if he was comfortable sharing his story, and reluctantly, he agreed. In front of the room, he told us he had been in Iraq with a Marine unit, when his convoy of heavy armored vehicles hit an Improvised Explosive Device, more commonly known by the acronym IED. The blast was deafening, and as he scrambled out of his Humvee, he saw that the vehicle in front of his was on fire. Preparing himself to save the passengers, he scrambled toward the vehicle, which now was engulfed in flames. When he got there, he saw the driver through the window screaming in excruciating pain, struggling to get out, but the blast had crunched the frame of the vehicle. Risking severe burns, James grabbed the handle and pulled at the door with everything he had. But no matter how hard he pulled on that door, no matter how he tried to lever it, he couldn't open it. James had to watch this young marine burn alive before his very eyes. He was helpless.

James told me that from that point forward, for almost a decade, he had carried the guilt of not getting that door open. He shut himself off from society. He quit leaving the house. He stopped functioning. He was unwilling to move forward in his life because he couldn't face the horror of that moment or the blame tied to what he saw as his own failure.

As he told me this gut-wrenching story, a thought slammed me in the head as forcefully as if I had just been punched in the face.

"Dude, you never left that ambush in Iraq," I said. "Not only are you stuck on the X, you've chained yourself to it."

I couldn't help but think back to my decision in Bethesda, and how close I had been to making some of the same decisions James had made. But I hadn't. Invictus. Overcome.

Since that moment, I've talked to thousands of people, military and civilian alike, who are stuck on the X—that place where the traumatic or devastating event happened—sometimes for years. There was the corporate manager who had been fired and had gone back to work at the same company as a contractor despite resenting it every day. There was the woman who came up to me in tears, telling me her mom had passed away from cancer the year before and she had been unable to move on.

At dozens of speaking engagements and coaching sessions across the country, I've been able to share the story of my ambush and how I managed, despite everything, to get off the X. I've been able to challenge people who have experienced trauma, loss, grief, despair, and even suicidal thoughts to not just survive the ambushes life has thrown their way, but to overcome.

This book is my invitation for you to nail your own Sign on the Door and say, "I will not be limited by the pain and trauma in my past. I will not be held back by the challenges in my future. I will be forged by them because I am the master of my fate. I will overcome."

In military terms, an ambush is an unexpected attack. Ambushes are often deployed in terrain that can trap you between canyons or tall buildings where the enemy can gain height advantage to rain devastating fire down on you. Roadblocks or debris block your path forward. Obstructions or your own troops block your retreat. You are funneled toward a single spot, a kill zone, the X, and from the high ground or position of tactical advantage, the enemy unloads their firepower. Their goal is to overwhelm you, to devastate you, to kill your will, to make it impossible to escape their onslaught. If you manage to fight your way through a well-planned ambush, it's very likely you've only done so with heavy casualties.

A life ambush is the same—a catastrophic series of events that knock the wind out of you, pin you to the pain, and forever alter your reality. You can't avoid a life ambush. The average human being will endure at least five major life ambushes over their lifetime. Some you will see coming, and some will hit you like an unexpected tidal wave in the night. And no matter how hard you try, you can't pretend it's not happening. Just like that marine who was broken from watching his friend burn alive, you'll never fully recover from a life ambush. Life ambushes come in all shapes and sizes. Some might be a grievous physical injury or illness, the unexpected loss of a job, a financial catastrophe, the loss of a loved one, and the highest level I have seen is the loss of a child. Even lesser events can become a life ambush.

You might have experienced a life ambush if you have ever been:

- overwhelmed to the point of shutting down
- filled with anxiety, sleeplessness, irritability
- rehashing shame, guilt, and anger
- buried in conflict, miscommunication, and chaos
- dogged by emptiness and a lack of purpose or meaning

And the reality is even if you don't identify with any of these, you are almost certain to experience these things someday. It is an unfortunate part of human existence that at some point we will endure suffering. Life has a way of ambushing the best of us. If you haven't experienced one yet, you need to be ready, because it might be around the corner at any moment.

But even though a life ambush always leaves scars, it also offers an opportunity. In my work with wounded warriors and people who have experienced trauma, I've found they respond to life ambushes in three ways.

When a life ambush comes, the first group is destroyed by it. They're never the same and never recover. They become paralyzed by the past, unable to stop rehashing what happened to them. Forever the victim, they use their ambush as an excuse for their own poor behavior. Instead of owning the conflict they've caused, the abuse they've put themselves and others through, the addiction they've allowed themselves to fall into, this group blames it all on their ambush. In the end, they don't just lose the person they used to be; they transform into a lesser version of themselves.

For the second group, the majority who suffer a catastrophic event make it through to the other side, but it's always a point of struggle. They go through the motions of their lives, content to maintain the status quo. Fearing further loss, they reject opportunities for growth and new challenges. They become stagnant, their main purpose survival, rigidly clinging to the person they used to be and never growing into something better.

Then there's a third group, the smallest group. These rare individuals turn their ambush into a launching point. Instead of being defined by their loss, they choose to define themselves by the challenges they've learned to overcome. Their resiliency empowers them to grow stronger each day, and the ambush that nearly destroyed them becomes the primary lesson, even the catalyst for the new mission of their lives. They are not overcome by the ambush. They overcome because of it.

This is the story of so many of the wounded warriors I've worked with. Like Tyler Southern, the young marine who stepped on an IED and lost both legs and his right arm. Despite these grievous injuries, Tyler married the love of his life and is now an amazing dad. A better dad than many dads I know who have all their limbs.

Or Mary Dague, a US Army explosive ordnance specialist who lost both arms above the elbow in Iraq. She came back and set the example for so many other women, only to be diagnosed with breast cancer. With a life ambush on top of another life ambush, she could have given in to despair, but once again she used the ambush to launch herself and set the example for so many other women to crush cancer.

Or Ozzie Martinez, a wounded marine who came home with post-traumatic stress so bad that he stopped going out into the world. His wife left him, and he spiraled downward until he was suicidal. Ozzie finally "got off the X" and is now a huge advocate for veterans and wounded warriors. He is back with his wife and kids and is a full-time student and a member of student government.

Or Natalie Lopez, who suffered a traumatic incident in Iraq. When she came home from war, she stopped living. She lay down on the X and let her soul disappear into the darkness. As she went through the principles of the Overcome Academy, I watched her let go of her demons and forgive herself. She recognized the power of her story to help other young women, and now uses art to help others. By the time she left our program, she had not only gotten off the X, she had launched from it!

This book wouldn't be possible without the amazing wounded warriors I have worked with who absolutely dominated despite their mental trauma and physical injuries. They showed me the way, and they continue to inspire as they overcome every day.

Many wounded warriors call the day they were wounded their "alive day." I call mine my "rebirth day." Our life ambushes launched us into new, even better trajectories. We didn't just survive. We thrived.

And my question for you is, Which type are you going to be? The choice is yours.

This is a question at the heart of leadership. How you handle a life ambush, how you handle any crisis, is dictated by how well you lead yourself and how well you lead others. If there is anything I have learned about leadership through adversity, it is this: loss and failure expose our weaknesses as leaders. If you're a leader in business, in your family, or just of yourself (and if you're alive, congratulations—you're the leader of yourself), then you already have faced or you soon will face a life ambush. How you deal with that ambush will either unlock your future success or limit it. My goal for this book is to show you what it takes to do the former—to not just survive a life ambush, but to become a person who will endure adversity, overcome it, and even thrive from it.

There are plenty of SEAL books on the market, full of kick-ass advice on how to win at leadership and life. Those books are great. I served with many of the guys who wrote them, and I've read all of them and learned from each one.

This book isn't about kicking ass (although teams led by great leaders do kick a lot of ass). This book is about losing as much as it is about winning, about failure as much as it is about success, because personally, I've learned so much more from loss, failure, and pain than I ever did from winning, success, and joy. This book is about what happens when chaos reigns; when a person, group, or situation strikes your life with such ferocity that you can't regain your balance; when your success that you've grown to rely on is pulled out from under you, and even your sense of identity is washed away. How will you get off the X? How will you recover when life comes to destroy you? And most of all, how do you overcome not in spite of adversity but because of it?

If you are in an ambush right now, part 1 outlines what you should be doing immediately. I'll guide you off the X, moving from paralysis, panic, and blame to acceptance and action, so you can start living again.

In part 2, you'll learn how to lead yourself, and we'll walk through the steps everyone needs to take to be ready for life ambushes and to take control of your life. You'll assess risk, commit to change, and build or rebuild a strong physical, mental, emotional, social, and spiritual foundation to combat that helpless, overwhelming feeling and hopelessness that plague everyone in a life ambush.

In part 3, you'll learn how to lead others after catastrophe strikes, how to rebuild trust, how to make and communicate hard decisions in chaos, how to stay the course to carry your team or family through devastating adversity, and how to launch from a life ambush.

Finally, in part 4, we'll walk through what it takes to sustain recovery long-term and relaunch your life.

This book is about going from defense to offense, taking the things in your life that are spilling your lifeblood onto enemy territory, as mine was spilled onto the soil in Iraq, and transforming them into the things that get you excited to wake up in the morning. To do that, it takes a no-excuses, forward-motion attitude that I call the Overcome Mind-Set. You must choose to never give up, to always advance, and to make the moment you falter into the moment you get up to press on anew.

And if you feel like you've already quit, that there is no recovery from the failure that you've been through, that you might as well stop trying now, let me just say that I've been there, and it's never too late. It's never too late to get up again. It's never too late to come back. It's never too late to overcome and get off the X. I have the scars on my face to prove it, not to mention the deep mental and emotional scars from some of my own failures. I know what it's like to believe you'll never be able to come back.

And yet, I've overcome. I believe you can too, and I will never give up on you if you never give up on yourself.

This is what it takes: you must choose to overcome. You can be a good leader, an amazing member of a team, have the best plans in the world, but it's the gritty, tenacious desire to overcome—and the knowledge that there is nothing in the world that will hold you down permanently—that will bring you through any life ambush the world can throw at you.

I believe we have reached a time in our society where quitting is not only encouraged, but embraced. If something makes you uncomfortable, you're entitled to a safe zone. Comfort is paramount; acceptance is assumed. When things get tough, we quit. This mind-set is the opposite of overcoming, and I worry that if we do not turn around this pervading acceptance of mental weakness, we will someday lose our nation.

I believe we are forged in the fires of adversity. We are made strong by the greatness of the challenges that face us. And when something makes us uncomfortable, that's the exact moment to lace up our combat boots, pick up our rucksack, lean into the storm, and drive forward.

Stay awake to stay alive. You don't have to have your face shot off to get off the X and harness adversity to be a stronger person and leader. You just have to wake up and overcome.

PART 1

SURVIVE

CHAPTER 1

GET OFF THE X

Sometimes even to live is an act of courage.

—Seneca the Elder

IN 2015, I WALKED INTO A DEVASTATING LIFE AMBUSH—A BUSINESS ambush that would destroy friendships, seriously impair my health, and nearly cost me my company.

It began with great intentions. A SEAL friend had created a memorial to honor fallen service members, which an artist friend of his turned into a poignant art piece. He offered the artwork to my nonprofit as an auction item to raise money for wounded warriors and the Navy SEAL Foundation. I wholeheartedly accepted, knowing my friend's intentions were to honor the fallen and their families, which aligned perfectly with both my and my company's purpose and mission. It seemed a win-win situation for everyone involved.

The auction, conducted by a third party who tracked bids, payments, and receipts, surpassed our expectations, and a business friend of mine and huge supporter of our organization ended the auction with the highest bid. He was so moved by the amazing story behind the artwork and the disparate military and civilian people that came together to make it that he asked to make a documentary about the creation of the artwork and the lives of the fallen and their families.

Through emails and verbal agreements, we all agreed to move forward on the documentary. At first things progressed well, with an $80,000 fundraising campaign to create the film. We also had the full support of the Gold Star families involved, those who had lost a family member in Iraq and Afghanistan. It was critical to me to have their blessing, since the documentary would highlight the courage and sacrifice their family members made in service to our country.

On the surface everything looked amazing, and I was thrilled at the progress the film was making. It was coming together nicely. But behind the scenes, Rome was burning. My SEAL friend and the producer butted heads from the outset, and their relationship deteriorated with each passing day. I was focused on my nonprofit growth and managing our quickly growing company, and I didn't realize how bad things had gotten between them. I didn't get involved when I should have, and while I was aware there were problems, I truly believed the two of them would work out their differences without my interference.

The film marched forward, and it was finally finished in December 2014. The film was great. A tremendous tribute to the artwork, the Gold Star families, and the different groups who came together to make it. Most importantly, it highlighted the need to build bridges between the military and civilian world while we work to preserve and honor those who made the ultimate sacrifice. We previewed the film with the Gold Star families, who expressed their approval. The finish line was in sight. It looked like the documentary would premiere without a hitch.

Then everything went to hell.

Because of his personality conflicts with the producer, my SEAL friend had lost confidence in the project, and he came to me stating that the project should not move forward. He no longer supported the producer in any way and wanted himself removed from the film. This move would have effectively destroyed the project. I was scrambling to save what I believed was still a great project, but because I was unwilling to take sides against the producer, my SEAL friend turned on me. Instead of verifying facts directly with me, he voiced his concerns about the project to the Gold Star families as well as members of my nonprofit company's board. He accused me and the producer of fraud and collusion.

For weeks, I had no idea this was happening. No one approached me to ask direct questions. While my board did ask for documentation about the film, which we provided in emails and receipts, no one came to me and told me there were allegations against me. I realized something was amiss when I found out my board was having secret meetings. Members of my own board began pressuring me to resign, and I found out about the potential for a pending lawsuit against me.

On February 19, 2015, I attended a board meeting and was given the opportunity to explain why I was potentially being

sued and putting the nonprofit at risk. The meeting was conten-
tious, but I stood by the fact that I had done nothing nefarious.
By the time it was finished, four members of my board had
resigned and I was stunned.

In that moment, I was reeling. What the hell just happened?
The remaining board members stepped up to fill the gaps, and
we were able to get legal counsel to help us sort through the accusations and verify the truth. But so much damage had already
been done.

Two weeks later the lawsuit was filed and the allegations had
been sent to the *Virginian-Pilot* newspaper, where it was front-
page news on the weekend of our biggest fundraising event of
the year. We were devastated that the rift had gone so far but
confident we would be completely and publicly cleared of any
wrongdoing in court. Our legal counsel and the remaining board
agreed we had all the evidence to win, but we were advised not
to defend ourselves or even respond to allegations publicly and
to wait for the court decision.

I tried to halt or stall the film release in good faith for the
Gold Star families who had been upset by the accusations, but
ultimately my producer friend and I could not come to an agree-
ment on the best way to address the problems and the release
of the film. I finally dropped my support for the film, causing
additional backlash, additional legal threats, and the end of my
friendship with the producer.

As the project began to unwind, sponsors pulled support
from my organization. I felt immobilized, alienated, and angry.
My world spiraled. I couldn't help but relive the ambush I'd
survived in Iraq. Although there were no bullets, I felt the pain

and devastation exactly the same. Could I wake up from this nightmare?

Every morning I opened my eyes and within seconds the heaviness of the lawsuit broke through my consciousness. Everything around me was strained by the pressure of the allegations. Things at the office were tense while we waited for our court date. As we kept losing support, I contemplated stepping away from the nonprofit—the thing I had built to do good and give back to my community. I wondered if leaving might save it.

But I was innocent of the allegations against me, and leaving the nonprofit felt like admitting I was guilty. I wondered what would be left to rebuild if I walked away. How would I take care of my family?

Looming above it all was my commitment to the warriors we served. As I thought through their names and faces, the heaviness deepened. My commitment needed to be to them first—not my ego, not my success.

I wrote out my letter of resignation, printed it, and went home, hoping sleep would finally come.

It didn't. I felt worse than ever.

SIGNS YOU'RE IN AN AMBUSH

IN COMBAT, FORCES ESTABLISH POSITIONS OF SUPERIORITY AND tactical advantage to surprise and overwhelm an unsuspecting enemy. A well-trained team positions itself on high ground, with superior firepower and violence of action to absolutely overwhelm and devastate their enemy. The goal is nothing less than complete defeat of the enemy, rendering them useless, unable to answer fire.

Most forces caught in a well-executed enemy ambush do not survive. The amount of firepower and devastation causes them to freeze and lose their will to fight. Most die on the spot where the ambush occurs. The ones that survive often have serious scars.

In the vocabulary of combat, this location is known as "the X."

Good ambushes are designed to keep you on that position until you can be annihilated. The only way to survive a combat enemy ambush is to get off the X as quickly as possible. To do so, you must recognize the ambush, find a new direction, and then get off the X and out of the kill zone immediately.

When I was shot in Iraq in September 2007, I felt firsthand what it's like to be on the receiving end of a crushing combat ambush. The devastation. The helplessness. The desire to just hunker down and hope the pain, cacophony of gunfire, and raw firepower would just go away. But after years of learning how to deliver an ambush, my team and I knew the only way to survive was to fight back and get off the X. That is what we did, and thanks to my teammates' tenacity and courage, we won the fight and everyone made it home alive.

Ambushes don't just happen in combat. In business and life, an ambush is a catastrophic event that leaves physical, emotional, and mental scars. It might be a health crisis, divorce, business failure, life-threatening disease, or horrific accident impacting you or those close to you, but make no mistake: it feels like you have been caught in a nightmare. No relief, no escape, and no hope.

Just like an enemy ambush, a life ambush damages almost every system of the body and often results in negative, unproductive responses. If you survive, you are likely physically, mentally, and emotionally wounded, injured, or otherwise incapacitated. You might be facing a medical emergency after you ignored the warning signs, believing you had more time or could just patch the problem up with short-term fixes. In a business crisis, you may be facing a takeover, a catastrophic failure, or a bankruptcy or lawsuit that threatens your solvency and reputation.

Anxiety, shame, grief, anger, and depression overwhelm your ability to take action. You might be alternately caught between wanting to hunker down and hoping it will go away, and running right into traps that further ensnare you in the difficulty.

Personal and professional relationships may be rife with conflict, chaotic or ineffective communication, and damaged credibility. The people around you may feel the impact of your crisis, and they may move toward you or away from you, depending on your condition and response.

You may feel like nothing can change, that you are trapped in your circumstances. Many people in life ambushes choose to self-medicate with drugs, alcohol, sex, or other risky behaviors to take off the edge or escape the reality of the crisis, further deepening the sense of self-failure.

Worst of all, you may feel empty and worthless, like life has lost its meaning. When you feel overwhelmed, helpless, paralyzed, or crushed, knowing something in your life has been irrevocably changed forever, you are likely in a life ambush.

For me, the film's implosion and resulting lawsuit were a

life ambush. My mistakes started at the very beginning, when we began talking about the project. Instead of getting everything down on paper, I made assumptions about people and their intentions. I ignored warning signs, like the conflict between my two partners. I assumed they could rise above their differences to deliver a terrific film. I allowed my attention to be fully focused on my organization, ignoring the rising issues with the film project. I didn't pursue or insist on clear communication at every stage of the process, believing things would work out.

All of the inaction piled up to make me vulnerable to an attack. It put me on the X, a place where I could be devastated. Surprised by the lawsuit and the contentiousness of the attack, I was overwhelmed on multiple fronts. I felt physically ill from the accusations, and I didn't sleep well. It drained my emotional energy, and I mishandled stress. I was challenged mentally as I had to process all the legal paperwork and jargon to defend myself. Socially, I didn't want to see people, and the stress kept me from being good company for anyone. Spiritually, I was in a negative loop of asking, "Why?" and I didn't find a good answer to give me hope. I was pinned to the X.

TYPICAL RESPONSES

ALL FIVE SENSES ARE ON OVERLOAD IN AN AMBUSH. IN A FIREFIGHT, smoke or shock may blur vision. In a life ambush, it is the emotional tidal wave you're riding that distorts your vision. Your heart rate is elevated. The emotional blast wave of stress incapacitates movement and clear thought. The noise and chaos make it difficult to hear. Every system in the body shuts down nonessential activity to put all resources into fight-or-flight mode and protect what's left.

Because there seems to be no way out, you may feel the need to collapse or seek cover, even if it means staying on the X. You may be stunned in disbelief or active in your denial of what's happened. Depending on the life ambush, you may have injuries that require immediate attention, but you feel too overwhelmed or incapacitated to address them.

After a loss, denial is a way to keep the full impact of grief away for a while. It allows you to process it incrementally. I experienced this shortly after my battlefield injuries. In the hospital, I tried to convince myself it was all a dream and I was going to wake up any minute and be in my bed back in Iraq. Unfortunately, that was not the case. I was in denial. While it might be a normal part of the grieving process, denial only prolongs your ability to start the process of getting off the X and keeps you from making progress.

Many people respond to an ambush with blame, lashing out at anyone and everyone within earshot. It's normal to question the roles of everyone involved, but while you are on the X, you're not in the headspace to accurately and fully evaluate the situation. You need a fast analysis to make the best decision to get off the X as quickly as possible, and neither finding someone to blame nor making accusations will get you out of the crisis immediately.

People in an ambush will do anything to relieve the pain and pressure, even if it means making the situation worse. When the lawsuit hit us, I started self-medicating by drinking to dull the pain I felt every night as I navigated the nightmare. Unsurprisingly, it didn't work.

Alcohol or drugs might seem to take the edge off of a difficult situation, but they can't help you get off the X. Resist the urge to spiral down the path of self-medication. You'll just have another problem to solve, as I did. I had to get a grip on that in the winter of 2015. I have strictly limited my consumption of alcohol ever since.

One of the worst things I see—and it happens frequently— is people get comfortable on the X. They become comfortable wallowing in their misery. You can get all the advice in the world, but the question you still have to face is, Am I unable to move, or am I unwilling? That's really what it comes down to. If you're unwilling, you've grown comfortable in your misery.

I've heard this story time and time again from families that have unexpectedly lost a loved one. Whether it is a parent, son, daughter, or sibling, when a family has lost someone, they feel guilty for getting out and enjoying life again. They've placed invisible restraints on themselves to chain them to the X. They're so devastated by grief and loss that they are unable to go on. They're not able to process it. It's like being severely wounded. I was unable to get up and fight back totally on my own because of my injuries. I was unable to get off the X in that ambush by myself. I needed help, even though I was willing to move. My teammates made the difference. Sometimes when we are stuck on the X in life, it's the people closest to us—friends and family— who have to give us that nudge or even forceful PUSH to get off the X.

THE OVERCOME MIND-SET RESPONSE

SEAL BREACHERS ARE SOME OF THE BEST-TRAINED BREACHERS IN THE world. We teach them to use everything from lock-pick sets to manual and mechanical tools and explosive and thermal tools to get over, go around, dig under, or go directly through obstacles. You might think anyone can blow up a building to get out, but not everyone can do it in a way that doesn't kill you or innocent bystanders in the process. Breachers learn which tools work best in each situation, and they learn to make quick decisions based on the time they have on target and the repercussions of each method.

But by far the most important part of breacher training is instilling the belief in our breachers that no matter what door, obstacle, or adversity stands in their path, they will get to the other side.

Locked steel door? No problem.

Reinforced concrete? No problem.

Over it, under it, around it, or through it, breachers embody the Overcome Mind-Set.

I've worked with hundreds of teams, companies, and individuals that are in the middle of an ambush or still recovering from one, and there's one thing that elite teams and the most successful people do: they get off the X quickly. They accept the situation, plan a new course, and move.

It sounds so simple, but in an ambush, you feel like you've reached the end of your physical, mental, and emotional strength. It is dark, hard, and lonely, and giving up feels like it will be a relief.

Bowing out might bring short-term relief, but ultimately, quitting brings the burden of regret. In your darkest moments, you have to commit to overcome like SEAL breachers, who can get in or out of nearly any structure under extreme conditions.

An Overcome Mind-Set means believing that there is no adversity that cannot be overcome. Those with a strong Overcome Mind-Set change their perspective. Severe adversity is no longer overwhelming. It's merely an opportunity to take a deep breath for mental clarity that then becomes a problem to overcome. Adversity turns into opportunity. The Overcome Mind-Set doesn't ignore the difficulties and obstacles. It sees them. Names them. And then it resolves to move through the obstacle no matter what.

Part of what enables you to overcome is the belief that things will get better. Over it, under it, around it, or through it, you will get out of this situation, and afterward you will be stronger than ever.

That is the belief that will propel you off the X.

GETTING OFF THE X: REACT

GETTING OFF THE X DOESN'T COME NATURALLY, AND THAT'S WHY in the military, we run highly specialized immediate action drills to practice how to quickly and effectively get out of worst-case scenarios. It's helpful to visualize, think through, and execute a process for meeting our toughest obstacles.

Whether you're in an ambush now or preparing to better withstand one later, knowing how to get off the X by running your own immediate action drill is invaluable for your and your team's survival.

To get off the X, you have to REACT:

- Recognize your reality
- Evaluate your position
- Assess possible exit routes
- Choose a direction and communicate it
- Take action

Recognize: To REACT, you first have to recognize the reality that you're in an ambush. It's only through admitting the severity of your circumstances that you can begin to move forward. Recognition jolts you out of shock and denial, and it can bring clarity to the signs leading up to the ambush that you either chose to ignore or just flat out missed. By reacting, you stop focusing on your own pain and misery and start watching things happening around you. Most importantly, you get honest about your current circumstances.

Evaluate: Next, evaluate your position. When I was hit in that ambush in Iraq, I was out in the open. There was nowhere to go while my team returned fire and attempted to retake enough ground to get me back to cover. In a life crisis, evaluating your position includes taking into account assets and losses, as well as the position and condition of others on your team. Even if you have limited time, keep the communication lines open, urgently ask questions, get multiple points of information, and gather a quick big-picture assessment of the situation.

While it's important to be optimistic when you evaluate, you need a BS-free assessment of your current situation. There is no time in an ambush for rose-colored glasses. You cannot take action with false or inaccurate information that isn't an accurate assessment of your predicament. It's critical that you're honest with yourself and build a team around you that knows they have to be brutally honest as well. Many teams and organizations have imploded in ambushes because somebody sugarcoated information, causing an inaccurate response.

Assess: Once you have a clear perspective and understanding of your position, assess your action options. You will feel utterly overwhelmed, and it will be hard to think in the initial blast of a life ambush, so identifying the best short- and long-term positions for survival might be a challenge.

In an ambush, some of the choices for survival include taking cover, attacking into the ambush, or flanking the attackers by moving to an advantageous position. You may have to fall back to reorganize, or you may have the momentum to be able to blow straight through it, depending on what is going on in your life.

Use the best information you have available to you, and identify the options you can take.

Choose and communicate: In your crisis, choose the best option forward to get you off the X and out of the direct line of fire. You can always reflect and reassess once you break out of the immediate impact or inaction. Even the smallest step forward is a victory over apathy and paralysis.

Then, if you are working with others, once you've identified a path and location to move to, it's imperative to clearly and succinctly communicate your choice to your team. Make sure they know what direction you are headed and why. They may be stunned, overwhelmed, and in denial themselves, so make sure they understand where you are going, why, and how you will move there.

Take action: Once you've communicated your direction, MOVE! So many individuals and organizations gather information in a crisis, identify a point to move to, communicate that they are going to move, and then sit on the X forever, waiting for the perfect moment. In both enemy and life ambushes, the perfect moment does not exist. It will never come. The time to move is now. Follow through and get off the X, even if it's painful, even if it's hard, even when it hurts. Even if someone on your team did something blatantly wrong that led to the ambush, part of your immediate action needs to include abandoning blame and self-medication as options while you are on the X and dealing with the crisis. Both impair your Overcome Mind-Set and slow reaction time.

When the lawsuit against us was formally filed, we were on the X, and secondary explosions were detonating around us. I had to quickly come to terms with a new reality that all our good intentions had been unraveled due to personality conflicts, mismanagement, miscommunication, and inexperience. I was facing allegations of fraud and collusion, and it was now front-page news.

I had to evaluate my position, and it wasn't good. We had lost the confidence of the Gold Star families I respected so much. I realized I needed to rebuild trust with what was left of my board. As I evaluated my position, I thought long and hard about what we had accomplished, my role in the project, and how best to move forward.

Ultimately, after much assessment of my position, I did not turn in the resignation letter, because I knew I wasn't guilty of fraud or collusion. The biggest thing I recognized was that I needed to own the mistakes we had made and to mend what I could. I resolved to fight the allegations and to clear my and the company's name.

Once you are off the X, you need to reassess, essentially repeating the REACT process to determine whether or not your initial action has moved you in a positive direction and has stopped the downward spiral. If your initial action has put you in a better position to keep going, great—keep pushing forward, communicating, and rebuilding. If your initial action isn't strengthening your position, fall back and pivot if needed to get to a better position.

Your first move may have been easier, but you recognize it did not work and now you will have to make a much harder and longer painful journey to undo the first movement.

This is where many people will give up. Don't dwell on the first movement or wrong decision. Only focus on getting off the X, even if it is your second attempt. Make the hard choices that will serve you better long-term.

In reflecting on my business ambush, I had to admit that I didn't take the time to be proactive in defusing the personality conflicts and differences. As a young businessman, I had trusted verbal agreements and good intentions instead of binding contracts. I wished we had spoken out to defend ourselves, if only to deny the allegations in the initial media reports. I had made mistakes in leading the project, including a failure to recognize the signs that things were bad and a failure to take action, such as creating the contract I knew we needed.

But after a thorough evaluation and fact gathering with my team, I knew there was no fraud, and I knew that the paperwork and meticulous records we had kept along with the threads of thousands of email communications would prove that. Months later, the fraud and collusion charges were dismissed by the City of Virginia Beach court system. Despite proving that we were innocent of fraud and collusion, my reputation had been damaged by the allegations, and no media outlet wants to print the story that proves there was no scandal.

At the same time, while I had led the company well through the battle, I had neglected my physical health through drinking and allowing stress to lead me instead of leading myself well. All of these lessons could only be articulated after getting off the X and addressing the ambush.

As you use your Overcome Mind-Set to get off the X, expect that you will have to continue to reevaluate, adjust course, and begin again.

There will be damage. There will be casualties. There will be pain. Recognize that there are no easy ways out, only forward motion, one step at a time, one day at a time, getting off the X.

CHAPTER 2

ABANDON PANIC

Most powerful is he who has himself in his own power.

—Seneca the Elder

HELL WEEK IS LEGENDARY IN THE SEAL WORLD, THE HARDEST BLOCK of Basic Underwater Demolition/SEAL training, or BUD/S as it is known in military circles. It runs Sunday through Friday, and you're lucky to get an average of three hours of sleep the entire week. It's impossible to train for, but I had asked a friend what advice he had for getting through it.

"Just make it to Wednesday morning. Then it gets easier," he said. I grabbed onto that gem like it was the greatest thing I'd ever heard. Here was my way to avoid ringing out like over 80 percent of SEAL candidates who never make it. The bell hangs from a yardarm in the courtyard for students to ring if they decide to quit. During Hell Week, it follows you around on the back of a truck so it can be conveniently close by and in sight at all times, calling to you like a siren to wayward sailors. But not me. I was going to conquer Wednesday morning, and it would be all downhill.

Hell Week began midday Sunday. It was March, and Southern California temps hovered in the high fifties all day, which could have been bearable if we hadn't been soaking wet most of the time. Our boat crews ran up and down the beach, in and out of the surf, each evolution getting more difficult as our bodies became wrapped with fatigue. We didn't sleep.

The only sure things as the days and nights wore on were the sleeplessness and the clang of the bell as man after man rang out to quit and head for a warm shower, hot meal, and blissful sleep.

As the days progressed, guys began losing fingernails and toenails to the wet conditions. Men in every boat crew had patches of bald spots where the inflatable boats had rubbed their heads clean. Sand grated and chafed against every crevice and surface of our skin.

"Wednesday morning," I said to myself through gritted teeth, running back into the surf, the boat feeling like a ton of bouncing bricks on my head. "Just make it to Wednesday morning."

When the sun cracked over the horizon on Wednesday morning, I breathed a sigh of relief. I'd made it. I hadn't rung the bell. I felt a surge of energy.

Until Wednesday wore on.

My relief gave way to exhaustion. The exercises were decidedly *not* easier. That damn boat felt like it was going to break my neck every time I ran and it bounced, straining the muscles from my neck down to my shoulder blades. Temperatures dipped down into the forties.

The bell rang in quick succession. Clang! Clang! Clang!

Three guys out. Headed for a hot shower. Oh, to be warm! To be able to close my eyes for just a few minutes! Nothing sounded better.

Wednesday night I shivered on the beach, cursing my buddy and his advice. He must have lied. My body continued to go through the motions mechanically, but mentally, each ring of the bell was wearing me down.

It would be so easy to quit—and so many others were doing it! Guys that were twice my size and strength rang the bell.

An hour passed that felt like an eternity.

Clang!

The BUD/S instructors were clearly unreasonable. They were being harder on our class than on any of the others.

Another hour.

Clang!

Thursday morning came, and boat races resumed. The surf seemed like the instructors had brought it in from the shores of Antarctica. We carried our boat into the Pacific, too exhausted to even brace against the cold. We maneuvered out into the break, the waves crashing over the side. The paddle tore against my callused and water-shriveled hands. My fingers curled in agony. I saw the team ahead turn and head back to shore. We were going to lose again. I dug into the wave, willing us out to the turnaround point, listening for our boat crew team leader's directions, which carried across the boat in a garbled wash.

We turned and began the push back to shore. We were last.

We wouldn't get a break. We dragged the boat back up to the beach, awaiting our punishment.

Clang!

Another one headed to warmth and sleep. It was midday Thursday.

Sleep!

If only I could sleep. The winning boat crew sat on the beach while our losing team took another turn navigating our boat through the surf. I cursed my Wednesday-morning "friend" again, vowing to punch him in the face as soon as I got done with Hell Week. *If* I got through. The defeat from losing races curled itself in my mind, and each clang of the bell seemed to knell my own failure.

Clang! Another one out.

Thursday night we headed to the pool for swimming races. I hate swimming. The wind was howling, and temps continued to hover in the forties. Our boat crew resumed our losing streak in the pool races, and after each race, we had to climb to the top of the ten-meter diving platform to stand with our arms and legs out. I was probably 125 pounds by that point, and it felt like the wind could blow me off the platform.

From the platform, I looked down on the truck with the bell on the back, and in that moment, I was done. I could not stand being cold, wet, or sleepless for one more minute. I imagined myself climbing down and grasping the cold, rough rope of the bell that would let me get warm. Then I could sleep. The wind whistled around me, plastering my shorts to my skinny, shaking legs. My teeth chattered, and I tried to move.

All those visits to the recruiter's office replayed in my mind.

They'd said I wouldn't make it each time I asked to watch the SEAL recruiting video. They were right.

Clang!

This dream of being a SEAL—maybe it was out of reach for me. It hadn't gotten easier for me on Wednesday like it had for my friend. *Ring the bell,* my mind screamed. I continued to shiver on the diving platform. *Ring it! Get a hot shower! You can't do this anymore.* The thoughts pulsed in rapid succession through my panicked mind.

Voices shouted from the deck below, but they didn't matter. Mentally, I was ringing that bell and heading to the showers. All I had to do was get to the deck below. This dream was done.

CONTROLLING PANIC

PANIC IS THE BODY'S NATURAL RESPONSE TO FEAR OR ALARM. A high-stress event activates the amygdala in the brain, and if the event causing the fear is not immediately addressed, panic gives way to a fully instinctual response. That response tells you to fight or take flight and run away to survive. It shuts down the decision-making section of the brain to reserve all resources for your response to the fear. That's why it's hard to think through to the best decision when you're in panic mode.

But it's also possible to bypass the fight-or-flight frenzy of adrenaline and heart-racing panic. When something catastrophic happens, the moment the pressure of panic begins to tighten, stop and take a deep breath. Get oxygen to your rapidly misfiring brain. Actively resist the voice telling you to run or react. Panic causes you to make poor judgments, so don't let yourself. While you breathe, look at the events as objectively as you can. What can you control? What needs to happen? Breathe, think, execute.

When you feel panic begin to rise, and fear starts to thump in your chest in response to a threat or offense, stop and breathe into it to clear your mind instead of rehearsing the negative, panicked messages that want to surface. Prior to walking into my real-world enemy ambush in Iraq, I knew we were in a bad situation, and my heart was pounding in my chest. When the initial gunfight erupted and I was hit, the pain and blitzkrieg of the ambush almost overwhelmed me with emotion. I had to control the panic and assess the situation despite my pain and fear.

Hopefully you will never be in a real-world enemy gunfire ambush, but I guarantee you will encounter a life ambush someday, if you haven't already. The mechanics and reactions in a life ambush are the same. You have to control the panic so you can objectively evaluate the situation.

In moments of panic, it doesn't matter how strong you are, how far you can run, or how quick you can swim. I watched guys twice my size and strength ring the bell during Hell Week. All that matters is how well you can sidestep those panicked feelings to make decisions and keep going. You can learn to manage panic if you rely on preparation, calm, and positivity. These three weapons can help you defend your mental state even in the most difficult situations.

PREPARATION

ONE OF THE MOST POWERFUL TOOLS YOU HAVE AGAINST PANIC IS preparation. Commitment and discipline can carry you through the most difficult days of your life, because they will keep you from quitting physically or mentally. When a life ambush hits, expect it to be hard. Calm yourself enough to control what you can control and ignore the rest. Don't mentally check out. Preparation can be the well you draw from in the moments when panic strikes.

No one expects US Navy SEAL training to be easy. I certainly didn't, even once I earned a coveted slot to BUD/S. It was the culmination of years of pushing myself to overcome physical limitations through football and wrestling, and my personal discipline to complete one more pull-up or dip every morning and night.

When I began my Navy career and completed intelligence specialist "A" school, SEAL training was backed up, so I was assigned to the East Coast SEAL headquarters command in Virginia Beach to wait until my orders to BUD/S in California were ready. I've never been a big guy and probably weighed around 135 pounds when I checked in to my temporary assignment.

While I waited for my slot to open, I worked for a crusty SEAL warrant officer who had been around forever. He took one look at me and said, "You're never going to make it through training. You're too skinny, and you're going to freeze to death."

But I hadn't come this far to look back now.

It was the end of fall, and winter was on the way in Virginia Beach. He saw my determination and gave me a specific task maybe to give me a reality check or a taste of what was to come. "Here's what I want you to do," he said. "Every day I want you to go sit in the Chesapeake Bay for ten minutes."

I was young and impressionable, but I was hungry to accomplish my goal. I knew it was going to suck. The water temperature was probably in the thirties.

"All right, I'm going to do it." So every day, I sat in the bay for ten minutes.

After ten minutes, I'd climb out red and freezing, and shake all the way back to my barracks room. I'd take a hot shower and go to work. The funny thing is that while I don't think it made it easier when I got to BUD/S, the first few weeks I thought, *This water isn't that bad*. That warrant officer's advice and assignment shifted my expectations. It changed my perspective.

The preparation I'd completed, from my sports experiences to the warrant officer's bay exercise, taught me what to do when I wanted to quit. Those difficulties expanded my capacity for staying steady in adverse conditions. When my mind wanted to shriek in despair and panic, I needed to remember that I'd survived the cold before. I'd survived physical pain before, and I could do it again now. Preparation creates confidence that you can draw on in moments of panic.

CALM

THE SECOND WEAPON YOU CAN DEPLOY AGAINST PANIC IS CALM. It seems counterintuitive, but you can project calm in chaos. More than that, it's essential when you are leading others to take a deep breath when panic strikes and control your voice and actions. Others will feed off your response. I learned this firsthand during a ship-boarding exercise.

It was a frigid night off the coast of Virginia, and we were conducting ship-boarding operations. Ship boarding can be dangerous even in the daytime, with multiple watercraft engaged and various grappling hooks, ladders, and personnel in motion. The danger is amplified when conducting them at night. On this night, the wind was picking up, churning the sea into ten-foot swells, a formidable obstacle that further complicated the exercises.

During one iteration, a teammate fell from the ship above onto our boat below. He was knocked unconscious, half in the water and half on the deck of our boat. We worried he had broken his back or neck.

"Immobilize him!"

We backboarded him and maneuvered our boat away from the ship to contact our helicopter support for the medevac. We packaged our teammate on the backboard and connected him to the helicopter hoist in the deep blackness of night thirty miles out at sea, the choppy water conditions pitching our boat and making the connections challenging.

As the helicopter began to hoist, the pilot lost his reference point with the boat below and began to slide back in the pitch dark. The wind and churning water further obscured our position, making it nearly impossible for the pilot to connect.

When the helicopter slid back, the winch line became taut and launched our unconscious teammate like a slingshot about fifty yards out into the thirty-five-degree water. We watched with horror as he landed, fully strapped onto the litter, and began to sink.

One teammate dove into the water and swam to him as I screamed into the radio, "Pull up, pull up! He's in the water submerged! He's under the water!"

Each second felt like hours, and I continued to call for the air support to pull up to get our totally immobilized and injured teammate out of the freezing water and able to breathe again.

Thankfully, the helo pulled him out of the water and winched him to safety. Although he was badly injured with a broken pelvis, he had suffered no back or neck injuries and would go on to make a full recovery.

After the incident, my task unit commander, Lieutenant Commander Erik Kristensen, pulled me aside and calmly and thoughtfully commended me for how I had handled a highly stressful, chaotic situation. Kristensen was a large man and a great leader. We called him the gentle giant. He often tried to educate us junior officers on everything from the nuances of writing more career-enhancing evaluations to having better leadership situational awareness while conducting land warfare or close-quarters combat.

"Overall, you handled the situation well, but I have one question: Why were you screaming in the radio?" he asked.

"Sir, he was going to drown if they didn't immediately pull him from the water," I said. "They needed to have a sense of urgency."

"Screaming at them didn't convey the need any more clearly, and if anything, it escalated their emotions. It may have caused them to do something other than what you needed them to do," Kristensen said. "Staying calm in the midst of chaos and clearly articulating what you need will not only get more immediate results, you will earn the respect of those around you for being unflappable."

Sadly, Kristensen would be killed months later on June 28, 2005, as part of the quick reaction force shot down during Operation Red Wings, highlighted in Marcus Luttrell's memoir *Lone Survivor* (Kristensen was played by Eric Bana in the movie adaptation). I will never forget his lesson of calm in chaos. Managing my emotional leadership is one of my hardest fights and biggest weaknesses as a leader, and choosing calm is always a win.

In a life ambush, raw fear gives way to panic as you desperately try to find footing in the midst of changing and challenging conditions. Especially in the early stages of an ambush, panic creates an intense desire to react, often without thinking, to lessen the threat, to stop the pain, to push away from the offending situation. Panic looks like running, like lashing out, like hiding. Its sole purpose is to get you out of the pain, even when it will cause greater damage long-term. Panic lives purely in the moment, pulsing fear and irrationality through your veins.

I'd let my emotions dictate how I reacted that night instead of taking a moment to check myself and think through how to remain calm and deal with the situation at hand. Everyone involved already knew the critical nature of getting that teammate to safety.

Managing your emotions might be one of the toughest battles you face after a catastrophic life change. Fear, anger, anxiety, frustration—they all leap to the surface unbidden. When you're weakened by an injury or loss, those emotions can get out of control and cause you to hurt the people you need for recovery and growth.

During the ship-boarding exercise, my instincts gave me good information: we needed to get our teammate out of the water fast or he was going to drown. It was serious and time sensitive.

I needed people to take action immediately. But I didn't have the understanding that my panic only exacerbated an already high-stress situation. I needed to project a clear sense of calm to help everyone else do what they needed to do.

POSITIVITY

THOSE WHO THRIVE THROUGH ADVERSITY DO SO BECAUSE THEY replace panic with the Overcome Mind-Set, and they build a wall of positivity around it.

After my ambush in Iraq, people often asked how our family got through the shock and aftermath of the injuries and recovery. My wife, Erica, was a model of calm positivity. She'll tell you she got the call that I was injured and began to make arrangements for the kids and all other household necessities, so she could get to Bethesda to be with me as soon as I arrived.

Erica was as honest as she could be with our kids and shared with them that I had been shot in the arm and hurt, and that I would be coming home. She didn't know the full extent of the injuries, and she didn't want to scare them unnecessarily. Due to the help of friends and family, the kids were able to keep their routines and school schedule, which helped them stay positive and calm. Erica knew our kids would feed off our emotional response to the crisis.

Before she entered my hospital room to see me for the first time, she had spent four days waiting to get in, maneuvering through the hospital's requirements and paperwork. On the day she finally got to my room, I said I didn't want to see her. I was afraid of her reaction. But there was no way she was taking a step back. She didn't know what she would see, what she would be walking into. She just knew she needed to come in with a strong face and figure it out from there. Whatever she felt on the inside she said she'd let herself feel and deal with later, but she'd prepared herself to have a strong game face. She committed to remaining positive.

I was terrified of that moment, tubes running everywhere, heart-rate monitors beeping, trached and unable to speak. My face was swollen, and my eyes were bloodshot. I didn't know how she would handle it. Some spouses in similar situations have walked away. But Erica walked in, beautiful as ever, and walked right up to me with purpose, kissed me on my mangled face, and said, "We're going to get through this." Her calm was a huge relief. It made me feel at peace, and I knew she was right. Whatever happened, we would get through it together.

While raising three small kids and caring for me, she kept a positive mind-set. It would have been easy for her to slip into complaining and negativity, but she resisted it. Erica chose not to complain or question why I had taken this job that so impacted our family. Never once. She drove forward, initially grateful and amazed that I came home at all, but then we both knew that blame or being angry wouldn't get us anywhere. We were a good team. When you surround yourself with people who are positive and always charging forward, you have a better chance of staying positive and motivated no matter how difficult the circumstances.

When bad things happen to you, you can't change the past. You can only drive forward. Quit wasting time on anything that doesn't help you drive forward.

Remember, regardless of the overwhelming opposition or adversity in your path, you always have the opportunity to resist panic and overcome by finding something positive. Always remember that panic can only control you if you let it. Panic doesn't change your circumstances, so don't let it keep you on the X.

When it's darkest, you need the most fortitude and best attitude, but unfortunately, this is when it's hardest to summon those critical traits. When you've experienced a setback, a loss, or a catastrophic event, you have to decide, sometimes daily, sometimes minute by minute, that you will not quit. The Overcome Mind-Set is a mental commitment to drive forward. The only thing that truly stops you from overcoming adversity in life is you. If you absolutely refuse to quit, ultimately, you will succeed. This is the essence of being successful—as a Navy SEAL, in training, in combat, in athletics, in business, and in any endeavor in life.

———

That moment on the platform in BUD/S, the wind whipping around my legs, the bell clanging in my ears, I had to make a decision.

As I stood on that diving platform ready to ring out so I could get warm and get some sleep, a thought tugged at the back of my mind. Quitting guaranteed failure. It was just cold. I was only tired. I could keep going if I remained calm and quit thinking it was going to be easy. As I thought about having to leave without a trident, I realized that quitting wasn't what I ultimately wanted. I wanted to be a SEAL more than I wanted to be warm. I wanted to be a SEAL more than I wanted to sleep. I saw the bell on the back of the truck near the pool and gritted my teeth. I wanted to be a SEAL more than anything. I was not going to ring that bell. I rejoined my crew at the edge of the pool, determined to keep going.

Years later when I revisited BUD/S training and watched a class go through Hell Week, I realized my buddy who had told me that it gets easier after Wednesday had been right in a sense. After several days of no sleep, everything is in slow motion. You just have to follow commands to keep going and avoid thoughts of quitting. In the moment, you feel like you're going a thousand miles an hour and that you can't keep it up. But watching it years later, I realized the reality was the revolutions *did* get slower. The rests between did get longer. It doesn't feel like that to the guys going through it, and it certainly didn't feel like that to me, but there was a perverse logic in what he had said. But even if I had been in a place to notice that, it still wouldn't have saved me from ringing the bell. No, it was my goal, and my intense desire to achieve it, that really kept me from succumbing to panic.

When you find yourself in a panic ready to quit, take a deep breath and remember the ultimate goal. Don't quit just because you are tired, cold, and hungry and doubt your ability to keep going. Quitting guarantees failure, which will be just as painful as enduring whatever hardship you face. Instead, rely on your preparation, calm, and positivity. Then, it's just one small step after another, one day at a time, overcoming each moment until you're through to the other side.

That's it. Don't quit. Keep going. You're going to make it.

CHAPTER 3

OWN IT

An ignorant person is inclined to blame others for his own misfortune. To blame oneself is proof of progress. But the wise man never has to blame another or himself.

—Epictetus

IN THE FALL OF 2005, I RECEIVED AN UNOFFICIAL LETTER OF reprimand.

"Ensign Redman has demonstrated a consistent pattern of bad decision making," it read.

I couldn't help but believe it was a Navy career death sentence. Being sent to US Army Ranger School as a result of that letter just added salt to the wound. I left for Ranger School with words of the reprimand echoing between my ears. I convinced myself I was the victim, that the whole situation was fueled by a personal vendetta against me. Bitter about the course of events that had landed me there and the extended time away from my family, I arrived at Fort Benning in February 2006. Instead of steeling my mind to endure the wintery conditions and the physical and mental challenges ahead, I continued to nurse my anger and replay all the reasons this wasn't my fault.

Ranger School is a tactical leadership school. There is no better school in the US military that teaches leadership and mission planning, but I was unprepared mentally to appreciate the opportunity to learn from the best. Things got worse as my bad attitude deepened with the adverse training conditions, unfamiliar gear, and the hazing from the Ranger instructors working to wear me down so I could be rebuilt stronger. As the lone Navy SEAL in the course, I received an extra dose of negative attention.

On the third day in the field, we had to complete a land navigation course. *Ridiculous!* I thought, having taught land navigation for two years as a training instructor. It was below freezing at 0300 when we mustered to begin the exercise. Instead of pushing myself to complete the course in record time, I arrogantly wandered around until daybreak, convinced I was good enough to finish the six-hour course in the three hours of daylight. I stomped through the dark lost in my thoughts, irritated by the cold and stupidity that I had to complete an exercise I had taught to others. Unfortunately, I had not accounted for the Army's lensatic compass, a device I hadn't used in a field exercise. I also failed to recognize a simple fact: the Ranger School land navigation course was no joke. It was hard, and I found myself far behind as I attempted to knock out all six points in the three-hour window I had given myself. When time was called, I had barely found the fourth of the six points, and even before I turned in my sheet, I knew I had failed.

"Damn squid got lost! Needed a boat!" they laughed.

"SEALs don't know how to navigate anyway," the instructors heckled.

The verbal insults kept coming until months and maybe years of frustration and rage finally erupted. My weakness in emotional leadership was laid bare, and I exploded in a ball of unchecked fury.

"Screw this course! Screw you! Kiss my ass!" I found my company instructor and said, "I'm outta here. I quit." The split second the words left my mouth, I knew I'd made a mistake, but I refused to pull them back and swallow my pride.

It was unfamiliar ground. In the SEAL teams, quitting is not tolerated. The entire training program is designed to eliminate quitters and those without the mental fortitude to push through when everything goes to hell. As I headed back to the barracks and away from my class, I tried to reconcile what had just happened in my mind. I had stared at the odds of regaining my career, and in that desperate moment, I believed it was out of reach. Before I started Ranger School, I felt I had a thousand-to-one chance of earning back the trust of my former teammates. Now I was convinced the odds had become a million to one.

If only that teammate hadn't sabotaged me. If only my command had realized I was trying to do what was best in Afghanistan. None of this would have happened if they'd just given me another chance.

THE PROBLEM WITH BLAME

IN LIFE AMBUSHES, YOU ARE SO OVERWHELMED WITH THE CRISIS, the emotions, the drama and despair that you naturally want to immediately find the cause of the crisis, the cause of the pain. So often, immature leaders will look for someone or something to blame. Blame is the easy out. It gives you something or someone to focus your negative energy on and absolves you from responsibility. And if you are, in fact, responsible for getting yourself into the ambush, it would mean a sharp blow to the ego, and so, in order to avoid that, you instead look for a scapegoat or an excuse.

But blame only allows you to protect your ego and your view of yourself at the expense of recovery. You can't survive an ambush if you're stuck in the past.

As I began Ranger School, I believed I was a victim and that people and circumstances beyond my control had sabotaged me. I thought, *I'm here because all these other external factors occurred. I'm a victim of my circumstances. Hopefully, someone else will come along and bail me out of this problem, or it will resolve itself over time.* We keep making our case, complaining and hoping others will agree that we've been shafted. The reality is we're really sabotaging ourselves and refusing to move forward off the X.

And what if there really is someone to blame for your life crisis? A drunk driver hits and kills a family member, or another company unethically bleeds your company dry and gets away with it—what then? Assign responsibility where it is due and get on with what you can control. Knowing someone else is responsible might make you feel better for a minute, but it doesn't help you to immediately get off the X. The loss or crisis is still raging. Blame can't change it. People who lose a family member to homicide will tell you that they direct most of their energy into getting justice after a murder, and rightly so, but even in the best-case scenario where justice is served, it doesn't restore the loved one. After the trial, they are empty and grieving and still on the X. The problem is not in assigning responsibility, but in rehearsing your actions through the crisis. If you spend all day focused on someone or something you cannot change, you are pinning yourself to the X!

Replace those negative blame thought patterns with the Overcome Mind-Set. The only way I'm going to fix the problem is to drive forward and create my own progress. It is on me to identify a path and move myself and my team there. Resolve to move, and figure out how to address the parts of the problem you can control. If you spend your time focused on how someone else needs to help you get through your crisis, you'll be stuck on the X for a long time, believing it's someone else's responsibility.

THE OPPOSITE OF OWNERSHIP: EXCUSES AND COMPLAINING

WHEN YOU ARE STRUGGLING TO OWN A MISTAKE, IT CAN SOUND a lot like complaining. Complaining is toxic to your mind-set and team.

My SEAL team was in the middle of its final exercise, known as a CERTEX, which is the final certification prior to deployment overseas. It was a two-week period during which we were running multiple missions every night. With the high tempo, guys were tired and on edge. The certification exercise was held on an Army base, and one evening in the middle of this training chaos, we were informed we had to move all our weapons out of the current armory into another armory. This is no small task, as the average SEAL task unit has thousands of weapons, from vehicle-mounted heavy weapons to machine guns, sniper rifles, assault rifles, and pistols. We were furious. We'd been told we would be able to use the armory for the entire training exercise. It would take hours of heavy labor before having to get ready for that night's missions. All of us were frustrated and angry, but we had no choice: the Army owned the armory, and the weapons had to be moved. All the guys were bitching, and I joined in, irritated that our time was being wasted with such a ridiculous bureaucratic oversight.

One of our warrant officers, a thirty-year veteran I'd known my entire career, pulled me aside and said, "Do you think you're helping this situation?"

"What do you mean?" I said.

"Nobody wants to do this," he replied. "We all know it's dumb, but you're the leader. Team guys are gonna complain. But it should never be you. Your positivity can turn their negativity around. But even if it doesn't, a leader should never complain."

That was a humbling moment. I was the problem. What needed to be done needed to be done. If you know you've got something that you don't want to do, just get it done. Sitting there talking about how bad it's going to be is only going to make it worse.

Ownership recognizes our own negativity and failure first,

and then it finds the people in your teams and organization who are harboring it through complaining, blame, and pity parties. Don't let complaining and negativity live around you. It will destroy your performance.

YOU CAN CONTROL THE WEATHER: OWN IT

IN 2006, JOCKO WILLINK WAS SERVING IN RAMADI, IRAQ, WHEN A mission escalated into chaos, and human error resulted in the death of an Iraqi soldier due to friendly fire.

Jocko tells the full story of this "blue on blue" incident in the opening chapter of the bestselling book *Extreme Ownership*, which he cowrote with fellow SEAL teammate Leif Babin. A "blue on blue"—when a fellow soldier is killed by friendly fire—"is the worst mistake a leader can make in combat," he told me from his home in San Diego, where he retired after serving over twenty years as a SEAL platoon commander and task unit commander.

Jocko is no stranger to taking ownership. When his unit returned to base and Jocko began writing up his report, he worked through all the possible reasons that had caused the incident. He replayed every second of the engagement, the communication breakdowns, the protocol failures.

In the end, though, he arrived in the debrief and boldly denied other men's admissions to fault.

"There is only one person to blame for this: me," he said. "I am the commander. I am responsible for the entire operation. As the senior man, I am responsible for every action that takes place on the battlefield. There is no one to blame but me." He then went on to explain corrective measures the task unit would implement to ensure it didn't happen again.

When I sat down and rehashed this event with Jocko, he described an unexpected outcome to his ownership. Instead of being dismissed or demoted, his embrace of extreme ownership actually built a stronger level of trust with the leaders above him and the men serving alongside him. Taking responsibility had not buried him. It had propelled him forward. Jocko retired from the military and started Echelon Front, a leadership consulting firm, taking the lessons learned on the battlefield and applying them to business. Since then, he has seen extreme ownership work in countless business environments too.

The leader's job isn't to blame; it's to own.

How much?

Everything, Jocko says. Even the weather.

The next time you get into a crisis, Jocko says, write down all the things that went wrong—stack up the reasons, the excuses, and every other detail that you think was out of your control that caused the failure. Look at the parts where you feel the most defensive, where you have the strongest urge to blame—what do you feel most like hiding from? Then, own them all. How could you have planned or prepared contingencies to address every item on that list?

Too often, someone defaults to, "Hey, boss, bad weather rolled in, and we couldn't complete the mission. We failed because we can't control the weather." That may be a legitimate excuse, but don't use it.

Instead, ask, What could I have done to control the weather? Nothing. But you could have come up with a contingency plan—

a secondary method that could be utilized in case the weather was bad. You can't control the weather, but you can control how you plan for it and how to execute in the face of such a disruption.

The next time you have a mission, and you execute the contingency that you planned, you will accomplish the mission. But if you know you can make an excuse, you won't set things up properly, or you'll only commit halfway, because you know you have an out if things go badly. If you rely on excuses, in other words, you will quickly become self-defeating. Worse, if you allow excuses as a leader, your team knows that excuses will be accepted. Instead of taking ownership and planning for contingencies, you allow the excuses to become a free pass to fail.

You need to take responsibility, but no matter what happens, if you're the person in charge, you *will* get this mission done. And when you commit to that, you'll find that the preparation becomes far more solid because failure is not an option. The leader and the team will work until the problem is solved.

This doesn't mean you're going to resolve to complete a mission one particular way and bang your head against the wall trying to make it happen. If one method doesn't work, you pivot and find an alternate route. But you're going to get it done no matter what, even if it requires a new plan and a redirection. Jocko's expectation that he can take ownership and plan for every outcome is the kind of mind-set that will help you move forward too.

FROM BLAME TO FULL RESPONSIBILITY

THE MORNING AFTER I QUIT THE LAND NAV COURSE AT RANGER School, I headed to check out, but first I had to meet with the Ranger School colonel in charge. In the colonel's office, he asked me to explain myself.

"Sir, I've been railroaded over some internal politics left over from my last deployment. I can't overcome it, because someone will always be there to throw it back in my face. I'll never be able to recover my career. It's not worth it. It's time for me to leave the military. I need to go back to my family."

I had lost my Overcome Mind-Set somewhere between Afghanistan and that land nav course. I rehearsed all the reasons I couldn't finish, the reasons my career was over, the people I believed had sabotaged me. I was entrenched in my own negativity and stuck on the X.

Sometimes in life, fate steps in to change your course. Some people call them God moments, some luck, karma, serendipity, but no matter what you want to call it, this next moment changed my life and saved my career. In that moment, as I was spilling my victim guts to the colonel, he paused to make a call to a friend of his, Captain Vince Peterson, the SEAL leader I respected most in the world. Captain Peterson had recommended me for the Seaman to Admiral program, and he'd inspired me to stay in school when I wanted to come back to the teams after the 9/11 attacks. Captain Peterson had spent his entire career defying odds, and by some force of fate, I was about to talk to him after I had just quit.

"Do you really want to end your career this way?" he asked.

"You can recover. It's never too late. You can control your destiny and your future. Give them something to respect, and finish this course." Captain Peterson then gave me the strongest leadership advice I have ever been given to this day: "People will follow you if you give them a reason to."

I listened. Captain Peterson's conversation that morning reframed my entire outlook on leadership from that day forward. I was sure I had thrown my career away and would never earn back the trust of my teammates. He convinced me I could earn back the respect of my fellow SEALs if I worked hard and gave the men something to respect.

For the first time in months, I felt a glimmer of hope. It wasn't too late. I could stop blaming others, take responsibility, and create a new future. Captain Peterson outlined the alternate negative course he guaranteed I would take if I followed through with quitting. I knew deep down it wasn't an option. Not as long as there was hope.

I had a new direction, even if there was more adversity ahead in being rolled back to the next Ranger course, being away from my family for another month, and having to prove to myself that I could come back stronger. I needed to stop blaming everyone else and take full ownership of my course forward.

You can take a new direction too, but you'll have to abandon blame and take ownership, even if it's uncomfortable. It's natural to not want to look weak. Sometimes you refuse to own something because you're afraid that if you own it, you won't be able to fix it. Or you know there's hell to pay. Those are just excuses designed to protect your ego. You have to drop them.

Ego is such a double-edged sword. On one hand, it drives

you forward and helps you feel confident in your perception of yourself. It becomes problematic, though, when you cling to false perceptions about yourself just to avoid pain or fault. When ego becomes arrogance, it needs to be defended at all costs and blinds us to the truth. You have to keep your ego in check or it will control you.

Take ownership in the midst of your life ambush. Plan contingencies for the things you are afraid might go wrong, and brainstorm a few extra obstacles to overcome while you're at it. You just might find that in taking responsibility for all outcomes, you discover the fastest way off the X and into a life you love.

CHAPTER 4

ACCEPTANCE

If you are pained by any external thing, it is not this thing that disturbs you, but your own judgment about it. And it is in your power to wipe out this judgment now.

—Marcus Aurelius

IT WAS HALLOWEEN NIGHT, AND SHAWN LOPEZ, RETIRED MARINE CORPS sergeant, watched as his two children, seven-year-old son Shawn-nee, dressed as a Red Power Ranger, and three-year-old daughter Mia, dressed as a zombie, ran in circles, laughing, excited about trick-or-treating. He was tired, but he smiled at their antics. These were the moments he'd been afraid to miss while he was deployed overseas. Now he was here. He wouldn't miss this one.

"Trick-or-treat, Daddy! Trick-or-treat!" they shouted.

"Yes, we'll go. We just have to wait for it to get dark," he assured them.

As dusk fell, they headed outside into the cool fall air. His wife walked beside him, and he was grateful they'd had a peaceful evening so far. He'd had a rough transition into civilian life, but that was normal, right? Some of his drinking buddies lamented with him on Friday nights that people just didn't understand how hard it was. But tonight, all was right in the world, and he beamed at his kids, happy to be a dad. Happy to have their small hands tucked safely in his.

As they walked up the street, the night sky darkened and took on an ominous orange glow that reminded Shawn of dusk in the deserts of the Middle East. Shawn's heart began to race. His eyes darted across lawns, searching the faces of the ghouls and distorted masks. Teens walked by, their face paint blurring and shifting from white to green and black. He tightened his grip on his son's hand. Some porches had flashing lights strobing out of jack-o'-lanterns, and kids walked up the street with glowing lightsabers and rat-a-tat-tatting toy rifles. He couldn't get a deep breath.

He released his son, who ran up to ring the doorbell at a house. Shawn held his breath, ready to pounce on anyone who might jump his son.

A woman in a tall witch hat answered the door and cackled, dropping candy into the kids' bags. They came skipping back to the sidewalk.

Shawn was sweating and visibly shaken.

"Shawn, are you feeling okay?" his wife asked.

"Yes, yes; keep going."

He wiped his brow and took a gulp of cool air. He could barely hear the laughing voices of his children. The night sounds were distorted and humming loudly in his ears. Suddenly, something flashed and he jumped. He fought the urge to charge ahead and tackle the next thing in his path. He turned in a slow circle, the lights, the costumes, the dark, the buzzing sounds all conspiring against him.

"Hey, here's the haunted house! Let's go, Daddy!" his son said.

Shawn took a deep breath. It was fine. He was fine. This was supposed to be fun, remember? he reminded himself. They walked into the dark entryway, and footsteps echoed overhead. A green-gray glow burned up ahead under a door. A thought pulsed through his head: he had to clear the room.

A face flashed in his mind, and for a split second he was back in a compound overseas. His night vision wasn't working. He needed backup. He stiffened, and his wife's hand caught his sleeve.

"Shawn?"

"Daddy?" His daughter looked up at him questioningly. Shawn shook his head and snatched her up, hugging her against his chest, scanning the room. His head began to spin.

"I have to go." He handed his daughter to his wife and ran home—trying once again to outrun the demons that had chased him back to the United States.

As he downed a drink in his kitchen, trying to slow his heart rate, tears streamed down his face. He hadn't cried once in Afghanistan. But here he was, missing another fun event with his kids because he couldn't get things straight in his mind. He knew he had post-traumatic stress disorder (PTSD)—it was impossible to ignore. But he'd downplayed it, thought he would get past it if he could just work harder, get some sleep, have a normal life.

It only escalated, and his attempts to self-medicate and over-work to make up for his erratic behavior left him hanging by a thread.

He stared at his phone where the picture of his kids grinned back at him. He wanted to be a good dad. That's what he wanted more than anything, but these nightmares, episodes, and flash-backs were unraveling him. For the first time, he realized he might not be able to win this fight.

The defeat was unnerving. He'd never given up. He'd never given in. He'd always charged forward. But he couldn't go on like this. Maybe they'd be better off without him. But thinking back to the street of trick-or-treaters outside, he realized he didn't want them to go through life without him. He admitted then, for the first time, that he was still stuck in Afghanistan in his mind. He realized in that moment that, just like so many ambushes he had been in, he was stuck on the X. His kids needed him to get free of that. He wanted to be able to trick-or-treat with them again.

He looked from the bottle on the counter to his phone. He wasn't sure he could choose. He wasn't sure he could face the past. He just knew he couldn't live this way in the present anymore.

ACCEPTANCE IS NOT SURRENDER

Shawn's story is not uncommon. So many who suffer with PTSD think they can escape the trauma of the battlefield or crisis by outrunning it or outworking it. I've had the honor of working with hundreds of wounded warriors. I am a wounded warrior too, and I have felt these same overwhelming emotions, left over from the ferocity of combat. I've experienced the inability to feel normal around people who have never been exposed to combat or constant violent threats to their lives. It causes so many of us to come home only to want to turn off the world, stay inside, and self-medicate with alcohol or drugs to numb the pain. I've watched so many wounded warriors like Shawn be held back by combat. Many are held back by the very ambush where they were injured or lost buddies. They refuse to allow themselves to move forward or enjoy life again, buried by survivor's guilt. They pin themselves to the X, ultimately refusing to accept that life has changed and they have to change with it.

Make no mistake: acceptance isn't quitting, defeat, or surrender. It's the beginning of leading yourself again. Acceptance is a radical recognition that your life has changed permanently and you're actively choosing to enter that new reality, as messy as it will be. You don't have to say that what happened was right or that it's okay, because maybe it isn't. Acceptance means we realize we have to live in this new state, so we begin to make adjustments to our thinking and actions to match that new reality.

You may be battling depression, anxiety, PTSD, or any number of difficulties after your life ambush. All of those are natural human responses. Depression is a normal response to extreme loss. PTSD is a well-documented response to trauma and brain overload in stressful and devastating events. Acceptance won't wipe them out, and it shouldn't. But instead of fighting against them with denial and anger, acceptance sees them and knows what they are. It seeks help if needed and commits to the long-term healing needed to move through these states. And the truth is, after working with hundreds of wounded warriors, I'm aware that we may never move completely past those scars. Stop letting eradication be your goal. It is not about vanquishing the dragon, in the words of a fellow wounded SEAL I know, Jimmy Hatch, author of *Touching the Dragon*; it's about accepting that the dragon lives within you now, confronting it, and learning to slowly touch the dragon so you can live with it.

Acceptance starts with one decision to move forward. Most people who are stuck on the X aren't making that decision. They aren't doing anything. They're barely living, going through the motions. They might say they want things to change or that they are going to make improvements, but no effort is made in their daily lives toward those goals. Sometimes people don't even have goals.

You may feel like you're alone, but you have to understand that you're not suffering by yourself. Adversity naturally creates an armor to protect you, but it can also isolate you so that all you think about is your own problems and pain. Wake up. Many people have it worse than you. Every day you get is a gift. Every day is a new opportunity to move forward. You're just wasting time sitting there dwelling on your depression and victimhood, just like I did in Ranger School. But it's never too late.

REACT

REMEMBER, IF YOU ARE STUCK, IT'S TIME FOR YOUR IMMEDIATE action drill. You have to REACT. Recognize your reality, Evaluate your position, Assess possible exit routes, Choose a direction and communicate it, and Take action.

After you recognize your reality, evaluate your current position. Where are you and what are your current obstacles, hurdles, strengths, and weaknesses? What is pinning you to the X? What losses have you incurred? What assets do you still have? Who can help you?

You may need to ask tough questions to the people closest to you, and be prepared to hear some uncomfortable answers. If you ask your spouse if you drink too much, lose your temper too often, or act erratically, be prepared to hear those responses and take them into account as you build your course of action. Don't make excuses; own them.

Next, you will assess the possible actions. There's not going to be an easy way out—stop looking for it. Even if you are under pressure, don't pick the first idea that presents itself just because you're in a panic or impatient to finally get off the X. Take time to assess the various routes out of your crisis, thinking through the consequences of each.

Commit to change and communicate: once you know what is holding you to the X, and you are ready to move, communicate your new direction clearly to those around you. Articulate where you are going and why, even if your crisis is personal and only involves you. Share it with at least one other supportive person who can punch holes in your plan and help you patch them if needed.

Then, take action. This is critical. So many people develop a plan and never execute it. They wait for the perfect moment that will never come. Stop waiting for the perfect moment. There is no easy way out. It's one grueling small step after another in the new direction. You are going to continue to meet resistance, and possibly consequences from your past actions, as you move forward. Use your Overcome Mind-Set to face those challenges head-on. Change requires commitment, action, and discipline. You've got to take the action to make the change, and then you've got to discipline yourself to continue that action until you've accomplished what you set out to do.

THE ROLE OF STORY

MANY WHO FIND THEMSELVES ON THE X ARE ASHAMED OF THEIR past, so they block the quickest routes to acceptance: telling their story. Perhaps it was an egregious mistake that put them into that situation. They'd rather forget what happened, so they sure as hell don't want to highlight it. But learning to explore, understand, and tell your story can give you considerable forward momentum.

The first time you tell your story is brutal, especially if your choices contributed to the mental and emotional trauma. It is never fun reliving a mistake or trauma, but by owning it, the incident can no longer control you. You now take control of it.

In the Overcome Academy, our intensive program for individuals who have been through a life ambush and want to regain their mental edge and begin a new mission, a number of participants said that telling their story was excruciating, one of the hardest parts of the program. Shame, guilt, anger, and denial had a throttle hold on many of our participants. We started with short, two- to three-minute opportunities for participants to share about themselves. Some only squeaked out thirty seconds. But over two weeks, they learned to trust themselves and their group to add more and more to the story they told publicly. In the final sessions, stories stretched into forty-five minutes. They got comfortable with talking about the uncomfortable parts of their story, and it kept spilling out, alleviating the choke hold it had held too long.

The more you tell your story, the easier it gets. You begin to realize that you aren't alone in your struggles and that others are fighting their own demons and failures too. When you accept what happened to you, it no longer controls you. *You* control it.

So many people have had a bad incident happen in their lives, but it still holds power over them, flooding them with negative energy. Every time they stop and think about it, negative energy bubbles up and pulls them down.

Once you reach that point where you own the bad incident and you control it, there's no longer negative energy pinning you down. Now, it becomes positive energy.

In the Japanese martial art aikido, you learn to take your opponent's energy and power and redirect it back at them. This is the same principle. You are doing aikido of the mind, taking that negative energy and turning it around, helping other people because of what happened to you. That's acceptance.

I've found that if you can accept what happened, if you're one of the fortunate few who survive a major life ambush and move to acceptance, people *want* to hear from you. They want to be inspired by your story. How did you do what you did? How were you so positive through it? People need to hear your story so that they know that if they were in the same situation, they could survive it too, that when their life ambush occurs, they will be a *little* more ready because they learned how you did it. Your lessons and courage build into your audience's ability to get off their own X and move forward in a positive way. It's not *weakness* to share your story; it's the strength of generosity.

That Halloween, as Shawn Lopez struggled to regain control of his body and mind, which was still in panic mode, he heard giggling and the hum of voices outside his window, a reminder of all he had missed—was missing now. He picked up the phone.

"Greg? It's Shawn. I . . . I need to talk."

He finally accepted that he needed help to deal with the demons. By the end of December, he left to begin his long road to recovery—to being the man and dad he so desperately wanted to be. He knew it wouldn't be easy, but he knew he couldn't keep avoiding it, letting it rule his life. He was finally getting off the X for good.

Acceptance is a process, not a final destination. Acceptance means you have decided to move forward—not that you are "over" what happened to you, but that you are through letting that event keep you stuck to the X. You will still have rough days.

Don't quit.

Keep driving forward.

And don't forget to share your story as you go.

PART 1 DEBRIEF

- Any catastrophic event that changes your reality permanently is a life ambush, and it can pin you to the X where you feel like you can't go on.
- An Overcome Mind-Set is your single most important weapon for getting off the X.
- In a life ambush, panic can derail your best efforts to act. Rely on your preparation, calm, and positivity to breathe through panic and keep moving forward.
- Blame blocks you from seeing critical information about yourself and your situation. Stop making excuses and own your crisis.
- Getting permanently off the X requires an act of acceptance.

- **Recognize your reality:** Describe your life ambush, including all the external factors that feel out of your control. Who does it impact? How has it changed your life?
- **Evaluate your position:** How have you addressed your ambush so far? If you haven't done anything, admit it. If you've tried things that have failed, record them. If you aren't sure, ask someone who cares about you and be prepared to hear some hard answers. Don't get defensive—take in the feedback.
- **Assess possible exit routes:** What actions can you take toward living a full life again? Write them down, even the ones that feel too big to tackle right now.
- **Choose a direction and communicate it:** Look back through your list of routes and choose one to try. Tell someone you trust about your course of action and ask them to hold you accountable for your action.
- **Take action:** Here's the hardest part: DO IT. You're going to make mistakes. Stop allowing yourself to be stuck to the X, and take the action you chose. Movement in life, and the first step toward living again, is taking this first step. You've got this!

PART 2

LEAD YOURSELF

CHAPTER 5

CLARIFY YOUR MISSION

If a man knows not to which port he sails, no wind is favorable.

—Seneca the Elder

MARK DIVINE, RETIRED NAVY SEAL COMMANDER, RECEIVED A PHONE call in 2007 that threatened to end the BUD/S candidates training program he'd spent a year developing and running with unprecedented success. Mark stared at the phone as he hung up. He hoped for the best but prepared for the worst as he thought through the time, energy, and resources he'd invested in his one-of-a-kind program.

It had started in 2004. After three years of heavy combat in Iraq and Afghanistan with substantial impact to Special Operations forces, Congress came to the conclusion that they needed more special operators. They leaned on the Department of Defense

(DOD) to make this happen. Naval Special Warfare knew they could not lower the standards, so instead, they looked to improve the quality of the candidates through a rigorous physical and mental training program prior to screening for BUD/S. SEAL training is infamous for its nearly 75 percent attrition rate, so preparing more candidates to pass was a great plan. At the time, only 35 percent of candidates approved could pass the screening test when they got to boot camp. The DOD turned to Mark to help improve the prescreening scores of BUD/S candidates, thus helping more candidates become SEALs.

Mark hired thirty-six former SEALs around the country and placed them strategically with recruiting depots. He hired legendary SEAL Bill Cheatham-Reed as the program director, and Mark took the extra time to travel at his own expense to meet with every single recruiting district to build relationships, organize the depots into boat crews, and instill the principles of an unbeatable mind, the mental mind-set he knew had carried him through BUD/S as his class's honor man (a distinction chosen for the highest-rated man in each BUD/S graduating class).

It took three to four months to refine the process and get the program to the exceptional level they knew would be necessary to serve the candidates and the contract. By the end of the first year, they were killing it. A whopping 87 percent of candidates who completed Divine's program passed the screening test for BUD/S when they arrived at boot camp.

The candidates were happy. The instructors were satisfied. The recruiters were thrilled. And then the phone call came.

Mark had heard rumors that the billion-dollar company Black-water, who had lost the initial bid for the program, was looking for a way to reopen the bidding process and win the contract. Blackwater challenged the company who had won the bid, the contractor who had hired Mark's company, saying the original company had outgrown its small-business contract.

It's not unusual for there to be a snag with a contractor, and usually, when a subcontractor is on board, doing a good job, the contract is deferred and assigned to the company who is already in place. That didn't happen despite Mark's exceptional results. Fleet and Industrial Supply Center (FISC) Norfolk threw the whole contract out and put it back out to open bid.

Blackwater won it.

Losing a contract worth millions of dollars stings no matter what, but in this case, Mark couldn't understand how he'd lost the bid. Their results should have been reason enough to rehire them. Who would staff Blackwater's program? Mark had all of his SEAL trainers on noncompete contracts, so there was no way any of them could have been legally listed on Blackwater's proposal.

Mark was given a ten-minute phone call with FISC Norfolk to ask questions. Mark had one: Why? Why did he lose the contract?

The guy on the other end of the line said Blackwater had a "superior staffing plan." After Mark got off the phone, he was speechless. He had thirty-six exceptional former SEALs already doing the job at a high level. His gut told him that Blackwater was going to try to buy out the noncompete clauses so they could hire his staff.

Within the week, Blackwater came calling. Mark said he was so disgusted and stung from the ambush that he refused to take their calls at first. Soon after, his entire team began to call. They were getting job offers and pressure from Blackwater. Mark was ill. He'd built a program that met unprecedented success with a team he'd handpicked. He'd had it all pulled out from under him, and he didn't know how to move forward. What do you do when you don't know what to do?

———————

Often, after an ambush, the course you've been pursuing is blocked or destroyed. Mark's company was making all the right moves, hitting all the targets, providing exemplary service, and despite everything, he was ambushed.

How do you clarify a new mission when your current one is destroyed?

WHAT IS YOUR LIFE'S PURPOSE?

IN THE SPECIAL OPERATIONS UNITS I WAS PART OF, OUR OVERALL mission was to be the most elite maritime Special Operations force in the world on the battlefield. As the highest trained, most experienced force, we got the toughest jobs, often involving direct action. Another word for *mission* is *purpose*, and our purpose was to bring the fight directly to the enemy. We loved it.

Under that broad purpose, we had individual *missions*, specific operations with unique objectives, parameters, methods, and requirements. Our objective on the mission in Iraq in which I was wounded was to capture or kill a high-ranking terrorist leader and take hold of all the intel that he possessed.

But in an ambush, your mission changes instantly. Whatever objective you had before becomes secondary to *surviving*.

The same is true for your life. If you've been in a life ambush, the goals, resources, and skills you used to rely on often become irrelevant. Just surviving the day becomes your mission objective. But after you survive, you often can't go back to the mission you were living before. Instead, you find yourself having to set a new mission, and this can feel incredibly disorienting, especially if you'd rather go back to the mission you were accomplishing before your ambush.

This is the disorientation Mark Divine was experiencing after his life ambush over the training contract. Mark was dominating his mission, but through no fault of his own, it was taken from him. He found himself asking, Can I really go forward after this ambush? And if I do, what do I do next?

And to answer *that* question, Mark had to go back to his broader mission: his life's purpose.

AN AMBUSH BRINGS CLARITY OF PURPOSE

IF THERE'S AN ADVANTAGE TO EXPERIENCING A LIFE AMBUSH, IT'S the clarity it can bring about what is truly important in your life. Crisis crystallizes your thinking, and you become clear about where you stand—often for the first time.

Mark knew this from the first time he'd course corrected. Before he became a SEAL, he'd been a CPA in New York. He didn't realize his life was misaligned until he stumbled into a dojo in NYC and began Zen meditation. He studied under Zen master Nakamura, who developed Mark's physical strength, but more importantly developed his mental and spiritual strength. It quickened Mark's realization that he was not in the place he was meant to be, especially after an audit that ultimately helped him define his values.

Early in his business career, he'd been assigned to audit a company that was being investigated by the IRS. A much larger company had laundered some bribe money through the smaller company he'd been assigned to audit. The owner was distraught and fighting cancer while trying to keep his family business afloat. Mark's small team began what would have been a fairly quick job, but his higher-ups dragged the job out for six months to increase their billing and revenues on the project. The business owner died before the audit was complete.

It didn't sit well with Mark. He realized the environment grated against him. He wasn't fully clear on a new course, but what he did know was this: money was not the most important thing for him. He valued honor and integrity and being good to his fellow human beings more. In the days and weeks that followed, Mark began to think deeply about his principles and the things he loved most.

He asked himself two questions that clarified his purpose:

1. What do I stand for?
2. What am I passionate about?

As he dwelt on those two questions, Mark began to realize how passionate he was about fitness and training, adventure, and risk taking. None of those passions were being fulfilled as a CPA. Mark realized he was living a lie, and he needed to realign with his life purpose. Through meditation and self-exploration, he realized he was meant to be a warrior. By the time he finished his MBA, CPA, and black belt, he knew he was ready to become a US Navy SEAL.

HOW TO FIND A NEW MISSION

YOU CAN'T CHOOSE A NEW MISSION UNTIL YOU'VE IDENTIFIED your life's purpose. After an ambush, you may feel aimless and adrift. You may have accepted that things will never be the same, but that doesn't mean thinking about the future will come automatically.

When I retired from the SEAL teams, I honestly had no idea what my life's purpose was. I didn't know what things would look like for me and my family. But I did know that writing the Sign on the Door and communicating my story gave me energy and hope. Whatever my life purpose became, it needed to involve creativity and communication. At the same time, I knew that I stood for honoring our wounded and fallen service members, and I was passionate about leadership. I had no clear mission yet, but I knew that those elements would guide my direction forward. Any missions that might present themselves would have to meet these criteria.

When was the last time you thought about what you stand for? When was the last time you considered what you're passionate about? As I work with wounded warriors, I've found that most of them haven't asked these questions in years, maybe ever. They're so busy surviving they've forgotten what thriving looks like. It's time to start asking those questions.

Passion is not about a vocation. It's about clarifying your contribution to those around you, to the world as a whole. If you are struggling to find purpose, I encourage you to consider what you want people to say about your life when you are on your deathbed. Will you want them to say you avoided life, that you were stuck in the past, that you didn't really know them or make a difference? Of course not! Instead, you'll want them to talk about how you made a profound impact on their lives by using your unique talents, skills, and disposition. How will you leverage who you are and what you have to offer to make the world a better place?

At this point, if you have *no idea* what your purpose might be, look back to your experiences and training. I once was told by the chief brand officer at Chick-fil-A that she was a theater teacher before she got into branding. When she was accepted for a job at a top branding agency, she asked, "Why did you hire me? I'm just a theater teacher. I have zero experience in marketing or branding."

"We've found that people who have a background in theater and teaching make the best branding experts," they responded. "You're a perfect candidate for this position."

Elite performers like the Navy SEALs train for thousands and thousands of hours. That training exposes them to a variety of skills and experiences, not just in combat but in leadership, communication, and even teaching, since often SEALs are required to pass on what they've learned to trainees. While few SEALs naturally think of themselves as teachers, I've seen them use their teaching skills to help people, both in the military arena and also in the civilian world. The *same* is true for the experiences *you* have.

Don't dismiss a skill or an experience you've gone through because it doesn't line up with the course you're setting. Everything you've learned and experienced has prepared you for your purpose. Don't let any lack of perceived experience disqualify you from what you were made to do.

CALL IN HELP

As you struggle to clarify your new mission, you might need help. When I was struggling after my catastrophic mistake in Afghanistan, I wasn't sure life was much worth living, and I was starting to believe the bullet in my pistol was the only way out. I'd never been suicidal. For me to even contemplate it rocked me to the core.

I didn't want to talk to anybody in my platoon, because of my mistakes. My platoon was already ostracizing me. Who could I turn to? I evaluated my options, and I went to see the chaplain.

Everyone needs someone in their lives who is trustworthy that they can confide in, someone who can be unbiased, like a chaplain or a counselor. I would suggest finding someone who's outside your normal sphere of influence. Who can you talk to who's not going to go blab your weaknesses to the world or make fun of you? Who can offer you real advice and maybe even potentially point you in the right direction?

Obviously, if you're stuck on the X in a major life ambush, there won't be a quick solution. But wise counsel might help you figure out the next steps. Maybe you need to get healthy, so you need to reach out to a doctor, nutritionist, or coach. Maybe you need to process grief, and a therapist or trusted pastor or chaplain can listen. If you need outside help to clarify your life's purpose, get humble and get the help you need. There's no sense in tethering yourself back to the X just because you're too proud to get help.

SETTING A COURSE FORWARD

ONCE YOU'VE CLARIFIED YOUR LIFE'S PURPOSE, YOU NEED A SPECIFIC destination to move toward. In land navigation, a general direction would be, "Go west." You can wander all over the place going west. You may never end up getting to your desired destination. Instead, a specific destination requires more information and better directions, such as, "Set your bearing for 282 degrees west."

The same is true for setting your next destination after your life ambush: it's critical to define where you're going and then heed the bearing to get there. In the military we have a group of individuals called point men. It is the point man's job to identify where we are going, the route we will take, the course we will follow, and the waypoints along the way that let us know we are on course. The point man leads the team on the mission, navigating the obstacles and ensuring we stay on course. You have to become a point man for your own life. Whether your destination is a business goal, health habit, or lifestyle change, your destination has got to be realistic, attainable, measurable, and adaptable.

While you're setting your specific destination, make sure it's realistic. I've found that most of us set unrealistic goals and timelines. When I was in the hospital in Bethesda recovering from combat injuries, I had unrealistic expectations and an unrealistic timeline. I wanted to get operational again in weeks or months. My expectations weren't realistic based on the scope of my injuries. In the end, I had to reset my goals based on what I could actually accomplish.

You might need to lose weight and say, "I want to lose a hundred pounds." That might be realistic depending on the timeline and your commitment to the process, but it's not going to happen this *month*. Instead, break it down into smaller pieces that can keep you on track—ten-pound goals, for instance—and that will tell you if you are progressing or if you need to reroute. Even better, focus on the behaviors that you *know* will lead to weight loss, since they are within your control. Those smaller goals are our waypoints along our route that let us know we're on course and that we're on the timeline we've set for ourselves.

Once you know your destination is realistic, the next step is to make sure it is measurable. This seems intuitive, but how many times do people set goals that they can't measure? If I say, "I want to manage my money better," but I have no metric for "better," then I have no way to know when I'm actually hitting the target. If my destination is to rebuild the relationship with my family or a business colleague, I can't just write down, "Be a better father, partner, or friend." Again, there's no way to measure that. I need to get specific and make sure I can measure the outcomes.

Because I'm taking ownership of all outcomes, as we discussed in chapter 3, I need to plan specifically for the things I can control and at least think through where things might not go as planned. This is adaptability. It means I have contingencies and a mind-set that is determined to keep moving forward, even if I have to change the goal. When I finally came to terms with the reality that I would not be able to be operational again because of my arm's limited mobility, I adapted to make my goal to finish my twenty years on active duty. And I hit that target.

Set your new destination and those smaller concrete waypoints and begin walking forward to stay off the X. Remember your mission—the things you stand for and those things you are passionate about. They will lead you and keep you on course, even if—no, WHEN—you run into further obstacles. This is what Mark Divine did as he made decisions about the deal with Blackwater.

LETTING PURPOSE REIGN IN ADVERSITY

After blackwater won the bid, mark had to make some tough choices. He sat down and meditated. He went back to his roots. He could have easily lawyered up and fought the decision. Several people around him felt he had a strong case.

But Mark went back to his purpose, visualized his future, and came out knowing that he would not fight it. He believed it had happened for a reason. "I was not meant to train people on a government contract. It would have chained me to a bureaucratic mind-set and shackled what I could do experimentally. I released all my guys from their noncompete clauses, and the next day, Blackwater hired all of them," he said, when I asked him about his decision not to fight it.

He had lost millions of dollars overnight. But because he knew his purpose, he was able to let it go and move forward.

It didn't take him long to see that his instincts were right.

Only three months later, while meditating, he had a vision for Fusion, which would later become a program now known as SEALFIT. The program was inspired by what he was trying to do with SEAL candidates; but now, free of the government contract rules and oversight, he could do it without anyone's permission. With Fusion, he sought to combine the best of functional fitness, yoga, and martial arts to build the whole person.

Mark launched a thirty-day warrior monk academy, a training center in Encinitas where he trained up to eight people at a time to be SEALFIT: physically, mentally, and emotionally. He ran it himself for two years until he realized he needed to scale the operation and brought in additional people. This freed up his time to focus on the team and leadership aspects of his growing business. Over the following years, he began an intense period of creativity. He wrote four books—*Unbeatable Mind*, *The Way of the SEAL*, *8 Weeks to SEALFIT*, and *Kokoro Yoga*—all within a four-year period. He said that if he'd stayed in his government contract, he would never have become an author or scaled the fitness company he loved.

"I learned that intuition is the highest form of knowledge," he said, reflecting on the experience. "It may be telling you to go a way that looks scary on the surface, but as soon as you move in that direction, you'll see it was right as soon as you look back."

Clarify your life mission and you will find that your direction is clearer than it has ever been. Even if you have to course correct, even if you have to pivot, even if you have to double back, movement is life and will keep you off the X. Keep moving.

CHAPTER 6

EMBRACE DISCOMFORT

Strength and growth come only through continuous effort and struggle.

—Napoleon Hill

THE SIGNS WERE ALL THERE. I HAD BEEN RUNNING ON EMPTY for months, trying to keep my company afloat while traveling extensively for speaking engagements. I had been drinking too much at night to try to relax so I could sleep.

After months of ignoring the weight gain, fatigue, and stress, I finally went to the doctor.

"Jay, I see all the great things you're doing, but if you don't make some changes, you're going to have a heart attack before you turn forty-five."

His words were a punch in the gut. My grandfather was a decorated WWII B-24 pilot who flew more than twenty-five missions over the European theater, earning him the Distinguished Flying Cross and seven Air Medals. Sadly, I never got to meet him. He died only a few years after the war of a heart attack. High cholesterol and high blood pressure run in my family, and my habits were threatening to take me down the same path.

I stared down the consequences of my inattention to my health. I was a retired Navy SEAL. I'd survived a life-threatening injury. Yet, here I'd put myself in another potential ambush, one that could kill me, because I wasn't taking care of myself.

What the hell?

The doc made recommendations for diet and exercise, but I already knew what I needed to do. The question wasn't what I needed to do. The question was how.

I stopped drinking and started making more conscious choices about what I was eating, especially on the road. Those were pretty easy actions. But then I started hitting the gym.

I'd trained myself as a SEAL with push-ups, pull-ups, and high-intensity interval training. But with my limited range of motion after my combat injury and countless surgeries, that regimen was impossible.

I was determined to get stronger, but my arm's limitations made me angry and frustrated that I was no longer able to do things that I could crush before Iraq. The more I focused on all that I couldn't do—how I couldn't do pull-ups, I couldn't do dead lifts, I couldn't do cleans—the more depressed I became.

I was broken.

I convinced myself I couldn't physically do what was necessary to avoid a heart attack. What was the point? Every time I showed up to the gym was just another painful reminder that I would never be as strong as I had been. When I was operational, I'd prided myself on my fitness. I was a fast runner and, for my body size, very strong. In boot camp I once set the push-up record doing over four hundred push-ups straight. In the months leading up to the Al Qaeda ambush, I was in the best shape of my life, routinely doing sets of fifteen strict pull-ups with a forty-five-pound plate. Post-injury and after the doctor's warning, I returned to the gym each day only to leave humbled and dejected. I would never be able to do some of the things I'd done as a SEAL operator. Every movement was awkward, uncomfortable, even painful.

My travel schedule kept me isolated, and it was a constant struggle to find a hotel gym to get a workout in after a day of flying or before speaking. I would often sit between sets angry and alone, thinking about my wife and my kids. I'd finish another mediocre set and head to bed, fighting the urge to order a drink.

By day, I was talking about the mental toughness developed in the SEAL teams, inspiring individuals and businesses to adopt an Overcome Mind-Set and push through hardship. At night, I was battling the demon that lived in my mind that said I would always be weak and a failure.

The doc's words kept crashing through my mind, adding to the stress: *If you don't make some changes, you're going to have a heart attack.*

I was trying to make changes, wasn't I? Yet nothing seemed to be moving the needle. If I hadn't been injured, this would be easy. If I had better range of motion in my arm, I could do the exercises I needed to do.

I would never pass a BUD/S screening test again. The thought haunted me—tortured me. I let that demon of negativity have free rein for weeks in my mind, undermining any positive motion forward.

I was never going to be as strong as I'd been.

That was the point. But it was also the point I was missing.

CHANGE REQUIRES DISCOMFORT

THAT NEGATIVE VOICE IN MY HEAD TOLD ME THE LIE THAT IF I hadn't been injured, then getting back in shape would be easy. It wouldn't. I was grossly out of shape. Four years of nonexistent fitness and a terrible diet would have given even a noninjured version of me an arduous road back to top fitness. My disabilities only added additional pain and challenges. I expected to be able to do what I used to do, and quickly. I was older, broken, and in terrible shape. Reality was choking me out. Some exercises would require new learning or adaptations to complete, such as pull-ups or cleans, but it wasn't my injuries stopping me from doing those things. It was my commitment to the self-discipline and discomfort that needed to change. It's a lesson I've had to learn again and again. What can I say? I'm a slow learner.

I had allowed myself to experience "freedom intoxication." No early morning meetings, no mandatory PT sessions. I wasn't surrounded by hard chargers who stayed in top physical shape because our lives depended on it. No, I got out of the military and began to focus on my business and allowed that and my injuries to become an excuse. With no military structure to hold me in check, my "freedom intoxication" allowed me to do what I wanted, which was...nothing. I was burning myself out trying to run the business and ignoring the foundation that would allow me to enjoy the success I was working for.

I needed to adjust my expectations and get back to putting in the work. The hardest part was accepting that I would never be as strong as I once was. For years, I realized, being stronger than I'd ever been before had been my goal, and it had motivated me to see what was possible. But reaching new personal bests every day couldn't be my motivation anymore. My physical limitations changed what was possible. Instead I needed to accept that I could do more than I thought I could. I needed to quit waiting for motivation to move me.

As my friend Jocko Willink says in *Discipline Equals Freedom*, "Don't expect to be motivated every day to get out there and make things happen. You won't be. Don't count on motivation. Count on discipline."

For those of you that have been injured or have had some major health setback, here is the reality: you will never be the same as you once were. You shouldn't try to be that past self. You are a different person now. Imagine your potential as a 12-inch ruler. If I take a chainsaw, cut out a half-inch portion from the middle of the ruler, and then glue the ruler back together, the ruler is now 11.5 inches. It will never be 12 inches again. That is the reality of a human body that has sustained grievous injury or illness. But let me tell you a little secret: you can ABSOLUTELY crush those 11.5 inches. You may actually be better than you were before. You just have to be willing to grind through the pain and discomfort to achieve your new 100 percent.

There is no fast track, no easy button, no shortcut to

self-discipline, but that's exactly why self-discipline is the best way to take control of your life again after an ambush. The hard part is embracing it. It's going to be uncomfortable, and you are going to have to get used to living in that discomfort if you want to get beyond surviving and make real change in your life.

EXTREMES: FROM APATHY TO BURNOUT

As you begin to get uncomfortable in pursuit of your life mission, recognize that there are some danger zones. I like to explain the phases we experience as we try to improve ourselves as the Pyramid of Change.

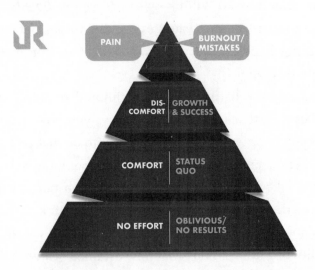

At the bottom level of the pyramid, there is no effort. Only about 10 percent of the world lives here. These individuals talk a lot but never find any success, ever. There are no goals, no action, and no momentum. People in this zone are oblivious to what's going on. People who get stuck in this zone often want someone else to take care of them. Or they might be like me after seeing the doctor—someone who is relying on who they used to be, making excuses for why they can't make a change in one part of their lives or another. If asked why they cannot take action, it is always something or someone else's fault. This zone is stagnant, and in some cases, you might as well still be sitting on the X. You aren't becoming a better version of yourself. You're likely atrophying. If the bottom of the pyramid were a location and age, it would be your parents' basement, and you'd be living in it after thirty.

Above the lowest level is the comfort zone. Seventy percent of people in the world live in this zone. They are perfectly content to maintain the status quo, accomplishing exactly what needs to be done but nothing more. If asked to do extra, they will do the bare minimum but not enough to get out of their comfort zone, and never enough to make marked change.

You will never truly grow in this zone. I watch people in the gym who are the epitome of the comfort zone. Many "work out" by taking a conference call on the treadmill. This zone is dangerous because as humans we want to be comfortable. And the longer we are comfortable, the harder it is to push ourselves, and the weaker our Overcome Mind-Set becomes.

On the other end of the spectrum is the very top of the pyramid. In this zone, comfort isn't the problem. No, here we're running too hot. Ten percent of people in the world live in this zone. I am guilty of spending a lot of time here. These are people who are trying to do everything but only making progress in a few areas. We're going a million miles an hour in one place.

They are sprinting on their first day of workouts to the point that they pull a hamstring. The defining characteristics of this burnout zone are mistakes, failure, and unsustainability.

Before that wake-up call from the doctor, this is where I lived my life. If I hadn't realized how dangerous it was, I might still be there. You have limited time, limited resources, and you can't do everything, but when you're in this zone, you believe the myth that maybe you *can* accomplish anything *if* you never stop pushing. It's mentally exhausting. The longer you run at this level, the more likely you'll make mistakes and eventually burn out. You'll neglect relationships because you're trying to please too many people. At this level, we're in pain, on overload, damaging our muscles, bodies, and minds. Many task-oriented hard chargers operate in this zone, and then they hit a wall and crash or experience injury to their body, mind, or organization. You aren't meant to sprint all of the time. It's unsustainable. You can't create lasting change if you're overextending yourself. You can't even impact the areas you want to move most.

To change, you'll have to set realistic expectations, which is what I had to do. At the end of that overload year, I realized I could not sustain what I was doing. I was damaging relationships. I couldn't take care of myself, my family, and the organization. When I lived in this zone, people used to ask me how I was doing everything I was doing. I would tell them I felt like I was a clown in a circus spinning plates on poles. I would run from pole to pole to keep the plates spinning, but if I stopped, they would come crashing down. And the dirty secret about trying to live at the top of the pyramid in this zone is when you finally drop from exhaustion, all your plates crash to the floor anyway.

FINDING THE ZONE OF DISCOMFORT: A NEW 100 PERCENT

JUST BELOW THAT UNSUSTAINABLE ZONE IS THE SWEET SPOT. HERE, we're uncomfortable but not in pain. We're pushing past the limits of what we've done before, using physical and mental strain to capacity. This is the zone of discomfort where change really happens. Here you're taking the necessary actions and implementing the discipline. When you start doing something entirely new, you have to put mental and physical effort into it, and you have to be disciplined to continue to do it. Often, it's uncomfortable because it's something new, whether we're working out, learning something, or practicing emotional control.

My injured arm will always have twinges of pain. Doctors told me early on in my recovery process that we could amputate, do an elbow replacement that would never let me lift more than ten pounds, or fuse my arm. Those were my options. We chose the last one.

They fused my arm and then later, we found Dr. Eglseder, out of Johns Hopkins and Baltimore Shock Trauma, who was able to rebuild my elbow and give me a little bit of movement.

"You'll probably never lift more than thirty to forty pounds," he said, "and you're going to have arthritis so bad that you'll need an elbow replacement, but I can give you ten years."

Since then, I have used the hell out of it. I've pushed through the discomfort, and it has made my elbow stronger. Sometimes I overuse it and it'll move from discomfort to pain. I've learned my limits enough that I know the difference between pain that can lead to damage and discomfort that will help me grow. By pushing outside of my limits over and over, I have crushed the

30-pound limit the doctor told me I'd hit with my arm. In the summer of 2018, I deadlifted 330 pounds five times. Only 300 pounds over the 30 the doctor said would be my max. Five times, Doc!

Now, obviously, if you haven't worked out in years, you shouldn't be doing heavy dead lifts. That's a good way to find yourself quickly at the peak of the pyramid. Instead, move incrementally into that zone of discomfort. Do it weekly, and you'll get stronger. Keep moving between the middle zones on the Pyramid of Change, and you'll be crushing your goals in no time.

If you've ever experienced chronic pain, you know how paralyzing it can be. It can cause you to think you can't do *anything* or you'll make things worse. But the reality is you can probably do more than you think. When I meet wounded warriors who are in chronic pain, I tell them, "You've got to figure out your own body. I don't know what your new one hundred percent is, but I can tell you right now that sitting there and doing nothing is definitely not contributing to making your situation any better." Never be afraid to ask your doc, "How can I take this a little further than expected without causing more damage?" Then press into the discomfort, finding that sweet spot between pain and growth.

In the short term it may hurt a little more, but it could also make it better.

Once again, it is important to understand that there's a difference between pain and discomfort. Pain will stop you. If you look at the pain scale from zero to ten, a one, two, or three is not really pain. That's discomfort. Those are the areas where you're potentially growing. You also need to keep listening. Does this discomfort eventually go away? If there's chronic pain, what are the other things that you can do? Is movement helping you? Are there nonpharmacological solutions?

This is what the Overcome Mind-Set is all about, leading yourself into that discomfort incrementally. Slowly push yourself just a little further. Measure it. Make it a little bit harder. See how long you can last.

You've got to quit being satisfied with the status quo. I have personally witnessed my SEAL teammate Ray Care squat over six hundred pounds. Ray and I went through BUD/S together, and let's just say neither of us are in our twenties anymore. And yet Ray is never satisfied with the status quo. He never rests in the comfort zone, on the gains he made in the past. He's always pushing forward.

One of the ways he moves into discomfort is by extending the *time* he spends in discomfort. In the fitness world, a normal set of exercises is three sets of ten to twelve repetitions. Ray pushes further, often doing *twelve* sets of twelve repetitions, meaning he spends *four times longer* in the zone of discomfort. But Ray goes further than that, limiting breaks to thirty seconds, often going thirty seconds on, thirty seconds off for thirty minutes. As someone who has worked out with Ray, let me tell you: your muscles *burn*. But at the same time, they never tip into pain. As anyone who has been injured training knows, there's no better way to wipe out all your gains than getting injured. No, Ray can squat over six hundred pounds not just because he knows how to endure discomfort, but also because he knows how to avoid pain and injury.

The point of this principle is that you can't do it all overnight.

If you've been through a life ambush and you're trying to get back on track, stop trying to get back to some mythical version of your past self, like I did at first. Start from where you are and define a new 100 percent. Then *incrementally* build within that zone of discomfort.

HABITUATE CHALLENGE WITH THE THREE RULES OF CHANGE

TOO OFTEN WE VIEW DISCOMFORT NEGATIVELY OR AS AN INDICATOR that something is wrong. Sometimes it means we're being challenged, and in those cases, we absolutely need to press into it for our benefit. So what do we do when we're uncomfortable? We build and practice our Overcome Mind-Set.

There are three rules to building an Overcome Mind-Set.

Rule 1: No quitting.

Rule 2: No mentally quitting.

Rule 3: Accept that life is not fair.

Rule number 1 doesn't mean that you will always succeed. Quite the opposite: you'll likely fail *more* often. But it also means that when you *do* fail, you'll keep going.

Rule number 2 might sound the same as rule number 1, but you can keep going through the motions, comfortably accepting the status quo even if you've never outright quit. No mentally quitting means continuing to press into the zone of discomfort. It means taking extreme ownership when you fail and preparing a solution and contingencies for that solution so that you don't fail again.

Rule number 3 means accepting that even when you do everything right, things might still go wrong. Even though life isn't fair, the Overcome Mind-Set stays positive. It looks for a solution, a way to make things better, a chance to keep pressing into full potential. The Overcome Mind-Set makes no excuses. It just gets to work.

To be clear, this mind-set isn't built when things are going right and you feel successful. Success is the by-product. This mind-set is built through failure, a refusal to accept the status quo. Instead, it says comfort isn't good enough for me. I'd rather be uncomfortable than accept mediocrity.

Related to the three rules of the Overcome Mind-Set are three rules of change:

Change rule number 1: Recognize the need to change and commit to it.

Change rule number 2: Identify the action required to create the change.

Change rule number 3: Continue the action until the change is made.

Commitment, action, discipline. Without these three rules, you will *never* create the change you want in your life.

Goals come and go. Once you achieve one and you start to get comfortable, you'll have to set a new goal, one that makes you uncomfortable again. This is an endless, infinite loop where you're moving up into your zone of discomfort until it becomes comfortable, and then identifying a new goal to move back into discomfort. And this is exactly where the people who are truly successful live their lives. They constantly identify new goals, and they get uncomfortable pushing toward those goals until it becomes easy. Then they raise the bar again. This is how elite people *stay* elite.

FIGHT FEAR WITH PURPOSE

PART OF WHAT KEEPS PEOPLE IN THE COMFORT ZONE IS FEAR. SO many people live their lives in fear, afraid to take healthy risks and embrace failure. You learn far more through failure than through staying in the comfort zone.

First steps to getting out of the comfort zone? It's time to tackle some things you're afraid of. If you're afraid of heights, rock climb or go skydiving. If you're afraid of snakes, head to the petting zoo and hold them. If you're afraid of talking in front of people, join Toastmasters and begin developing your speaking skills. Confront fear head-on.

It's the same in physical training, and I believe physical training is one of the greatest places you can push yourself out of your comfort zone and build an Overcome Mind-Set. And there are added benefits: you will look better, feel better, and live longer. (You will probably have more sex too as a by-product, which I am told by business-expert friends is one of three things that motivates people to change, so . . . you're welcome.)

The bottom line: you have to push yourself out of your comfort zone. I started doing CrossFit a couple of years ago because it is hard and pushed me outside of my comfort zone. If you find the right gym with the right coaches, they will push you appropriately to help you grow by getting into a healthy zone of discomfort.

Do you have a limitation that keeps you from being able to work out? So what? You have a limitation. That doesn't mean you can't do anything. It means you have to figure out how to get out there and push yourself to find your new 100 percent. My friend Tyler Southern is a triple amputee, and the good arm he has was severely damaged to the point that he is lucky he is not a quadruple amputee. Tyler is in the gym almost every day. He does modified workouts. Tyler is now raising two beautiful kids with his lovely wife, Ashley, and he never lets his injuries stop him. He just figures out how he can do it on his own.

I'll never forget the picture Tyler sent a few years ago after he finally learned to change his child's diaper. "One nub, one jacked-up hand, and my teeth but I did it!" he said.

That's getting outside your comfort zone and building an Overcome Mind-Set!

Once you've been through a life ambush, it's so easy to look back at where you were in the past and think, *Getting back there is my goal.*

It isn't. It *can't* be. Age, injury, and catastrophic events or illness all take a toll. Tyler is a shining example of that. You have to figure out what your new 100 percent is and build on it.

For months, I made those excuses. I said I couldn't work out the way I used to. I'm broken, I'm too busy, I can't bend my arm—I had plenty of justifications. I was partially right—I wouldn't regain the level of fitness that I had as an active-duty Navy SEAL. I can no longer fully bend or extend my elbow, and I have nerve damage in my left hand, which causes limitations. But I've decided I'll never sit on the sidelines again. I deadlift with a special strap to hold the bar with my weak left hand. I do jacked-up pull-ups that compensate for my limited range of motion. I have to do a modified clean, but I do it. And YOU can too! Once you reach your new 100 percent, reset the standard and push yourself a little further.

Elite performers recognize that there's an infinite loop that keeps returning to the zone of discomfort. The elite never settle, and neither can you. Embrace discomfort and let it make you stronger—one action, one day, one habit at a time.

CHAPTER 7

PENTAGON OF PEAK PERFORMANCE

The ability to lead yourself to success starts with change.

—Jason Redman

AN ANCIENT SAMURAI MASTER WAS TEACHING HIS FINAL CLASS. HE stood in front of his warrior students to deliver his final lesson.

"Will you be ready?" he asked them simply.

The students lined up before him in their traditional *seiza* position and thought about their master's question. One of his most esteemed students stood up and bowed.

"Great Sensei . . . for what?" he said.

The sensei looked at the class.

"Exactly."

If you only read one chapter in this book, read this one. You don't know what ambushes you'll face, but they are coming.

Will you be ready?

Your life is an amazing journey, filled with highs and lows and successes and failures in business and life. But make no mistake. It's going to go catastrophically wrong. If you are not in a life ambush right now, there's one out there waiting for you. This is the chapter that will prepare you for that moment.

After my enemy ambush and subsequent severe injuries, people were amazed at how quickly I bounced back. I became known as the Overcome guy and kept relentlessly driving forward. From the Sign on the Door to creating a nonprofit, to building a speaking business, to getting myself back in top physical shape despite physical limitations, I have continued to overcome.

Friends and even fellow warriors would say to me, "It's awesome you're driving forward, but I'm here for you when the depression sets in," or "Keep trying to crush it, but the bottom will eventually fall out."

Doctors used to ask me how I was so driven. I couldn't fully answer those questions back then.

Thankfully over the last twelve years, I have had ample time to reflect on the human spirit. I've had time to reflect on the Overcome Mind-Set and what it takes to build it. Most importantly, I've come to realize why I was able to launch from what should have been the most devastating ambush of my life and thrive and excel from it.

While reflecting on my failures and why I was able to navigate some better than others, I came to a startling revelation. There are five key areas in which people need to lead themselves in order to be truly exceptional leaders and find balance and success in this life. Those five areas are physical leadership, mental leadership, emotional leadership, social leadership, and spiritual leadership.

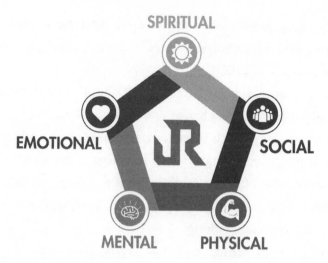

SPIRITUAL

EMOTIONAL

SOCIAL

MENTAL   PHYSICAL

I call them the Pentagon of Peak Performance. Before my combat ambush, I was rock solid in all five areas of the pentagon, which helped me survive and make an astonishing recovery. Each time I have found myself in a life ambush since, I've realized that I've allowed myself to slide in one or more of the five areas, which has kept me from being ready to meet the challenge.

This chapter will teach you how to apply the Pentagon of Peak Performance to your life so that not only will you survive future life ambushes, you will be prepared for them when they come. If you take time to build yourself in all five areas of the pentagon, you *will* be ready to face any challenge and overcome.

Too often people neglect one or more of these areas, or worse, refuse to lead in *any* of them and drift along completely unprepared for what life will throw their way. But when people aren't strong in their pentagon, they set themselves up for devastation when a health crisis arises or a business venture deteriorates. They have no foundation, so they crumble.

How well do you lead yourself? If you can't effectively lead yourself, you'll never lead anyone else. It's time to put your Overcome Mind-Set to work and get in the zone of discomfort to build these five areas daily.

As we dive into these five areas, think about them like a table. If your table only has one leg, it can't stand. The same is true if it only has two legs. With three legs, the table can stand up, but it's easy to push over. A table with four legs is pretty solid and takes considerable effort to overturn. But a strong and balanced table with five legs is almost impossible to overturn. It is ready for anything that comes along.

Time to get your Pentagon of Peak Performance on!

PHYSICAL LEADERSHIP

WHEN I WAS WOUNDED, I WAS IN THE BEST SHAPE OF MY LIFE. I WAS training to go to a next-tier SEAL unit. In Iraq, I maintained a very simple existence. I worked out, I operated, and I slept. There was a very tough physical screening as part of that evolution to go to the next level. The screening included a series of assessments, and the physical test is focused on functional strength with a run, swim, push-ups, pull-ups, sit-ups, and additional strength tests. During my time in Iraq prior to my injuries, we were mostly stationed at the main base at Fallujah. We were able to eat in the dining facility usually three, if not four, times a day. Good nutrition, good fitness, and good sleep. As I prepared for this grueling physical test, I was in the best shape of my life.

When I was shot, I lost four units of blood. The average human body only carries eight to twelve units. The doctors told me it's a miracle I survived with the amount of blood I lost.

"Your fitness saved your life," they said. "You've maintained such a high level of physical fitness that your body was able to withstand a massive shock to the system that would kill most people."

Most people treat physical fitness as something to preserve quality of life or prolong it. But for me, my fitness level didn't just prolong my life. It *saved* it. If you're ignoring your physical health, you're in denial about the risks you are unnecessarily taking.

There is a reason the foundational level of the Pentagon of Peak Performance is physical. Everything you do is built on your health. Your ability to move, function, have energy, have amazing sex, endure stress, and stave off sickness and disease is dependent on your physical health, yet so many do nothing in this area: terrible diets, horrible sleep patterns, excessive alcohol, drug use, and no fitness routine whatsoever.

America is the most obese country in the world. Because of our obesity, we have people chronically stressed out and lacking energy to get through the average workday. They go home and have nothing left to give. These people fall onto the couch for a processed microwave meal, hours of TV to dull the boredom, alcohol to dull the pain, and several hours of unfulfilling sleep before they do it again the next day.

We are seeing epidemic cancer, cardiac disease, and diabetes. In the next ten years, one in every three Americans will likely have type 2 diabetes, since research suggests that one in three Americans is already prediabetic. The next time you're out in public, look to the right and left of you. One of you is going to have diabetes if you don't make some changes. Welcome to your wake-up call. Stop making excuses and get serious about strengthening the base of your Pentagon of Peak Performance. No one who is operating at an elite level long-term is ignoring their health—in business or life. Physical fitness is not just about being ripped or strong; it is about having the energy needed to lead.

Physical fitness is the base. Everything is supported by this base. Your body is the only body you get, so taking care of it through good fuel, exercise, and recovery is critical to everything you do in life. If this machine you walk around in fails or does not work, then everything else you do is for naught. One of the greatest things about physical training is it helps build the Overcome Mind-Set and will make you more disciplined.

How do you begin? Honestly assess your current condition. Buy a blood pressure machine or have your blood pressure and resting heart rate checked at the doctor's office. Blood pressure is a key predictor of catastrophic medical issues. Leaders don't sit in denial. If you have health risks, you're not ready. Talk with your doctor about your current habits and how you can better fuel and train your body. If you've been neglecting your health, prepare to face some hard truths. You can deal with the health risks once you know what they are. Living in denial or refusing to go to the doctor because you are afraid of what you may find out is ludicrous. Get off the X and get that baseline medical assessment so you know what you are working with.

Once you have that baseline, stop looking for shortcuts. Forget fad diets and extreme calorie-restriction programs. You're going to have to figure out the best way to eat to fuel your body. More than likely, it will include limiting or eliminating processed junk and getting back to real food. Pay attention to how you feel throughout the day as you fuel, and resist the urge for quick-fix sugary blasts or caffeine hits. Use your Overcome Mind-Set to remind yourself that good fuel results in a stronger base to support all the other goals you want to meet.

Movement is life. I make it a priority to work out, because I feel better and have more energy when I do. I'm ready to face any challenge. Don't know where to start? Join a YMCA. They are probably the best value, because not only do they have weights, cardio rooms, and pools for swimming, they have coaches who can help develop a fitness program for you. If you have the money, I'd highly recommend a personal coach, like my friend Ray Care in Virginia or Andy Sziraki in South Florida. If you are looking for a group workout environment, Fit Body Boot Camp is a phenomenal training program where you get to work out with like-minded individuals pushing themselves to achieve their goals, and work with coaches to help you achieve yours.

Whatever program you decide to follow, set goals and track them, so you will know when you're making gains. Buy a heart rate monitor and use it during your workouts. Over time, you will see your heart rate decrease, and you'll be able to measure how quickly you recover from workouts. Additionally, there are a number of apps to help track your fitness, including MyFitnessPal for nutrition tracking and Strong for strength training.

Finally, don't ignore recovery time. Some people brag about getting by on four hours of sleep. The human body cannot work optimally on that little sleep for long. Instead, make sure you prioritize recovery, both in switching workouts to rest muscle groups and in getting enough sleep for your brain and body to recover and heal.

I talked to retired Admiral Bill McRaven, and he told me a story about how he prioritized sleep, even in a battle zone. The first couple of rotations he did in Iraq, he and his team would do five or six months, come back stateside for a month or so, and then return to Iraq for another five to six months. The first time he was there as a deputy, he only averaged four hours of sleep a night.

You're in the fight, pushing hard. It's supposed to be this way, he thought.

But when he took over command of the Joint Special Operations Command, he made a conscious decision to get six hours of sleep a night. The operators would often be up all night on missions and then come in and sleep into midmorning, but McRaven had to be up to talk to DC at 6. He realized he couldn't stay up all night, get a few hours of sleep, and then expect to make the best decisions with a clear mind.

"I told my guys that I was leaving the Joint Operations Center at 23:30 each night unless we had a hostage situation or a mission had gone south and needed constant monitoring. They knew what to do and when to wake me if needed. I had to have that sleep to be in optimum condition. Sometimes guys would give me good-natured flack about it, asking if I'd gotten my beauty rest, but I didn't care. They needed to see me taking time to rest. They needed to see that sleep is a weapon and critical part of readiness."

For so many people I have worked with and coached, taking

control of their physical health is the place where their Overcome Mind-Set is not only put to the test, but made stronger. They've lived with excuses and half-hearted effort for so long, just surviving their trauma, and taking control of their lives means baby steps into better health. When you eat well, work out, and sleep well, you can better handle stress.

Take care of the base first.

MENTAL LEADERSHIP

THE WAY TO BUILD YOUR MENTAL PLATFORM IS BY FOCUSING ON developing your mind. Brawn can win short fights, but brains and knowledge win the war.

You build mental leadership through broadening your perspective, increasing your knowledge, and getting outside of your comfort zone. I sustained a minor traumatic brain injury (TBI) when I was shot in the face, so I have been driven to improve my mental muscles and brain functioning. I know I have a harder time focusing than I used to, so I need to do a better job of structuring my focus and reducing distractions to get things done. I also recognize the impact of alcohol on my damaged brain, so I have cut out almost all alcohol. If I do drink, it is only on nights when I don't have anything going on the next day. You have to plan for mental success.

I had the opportunity to go out to the Brain Treatment Center in California for a month in 2017 and learn all about how the brain works. If you work out like a maniac at the gym, you are building strong physical leadership, but if you are doing nothing to push your mental muscles, you are only working half

OVERCOME

of the foundational levels. At the bare minimum, you should be reading and constantly seeking knowledge to exercise your brain. Your brain is a muscle that wants to be pushed. It craves challenge.

The best exercises that challenge the mind require you to use both hemispheres of the brain. An interesting recommendation from the Brain Center was to find a sport that requires balance, like paddle boarding, surfing, or even cycling. These exercises are great for mental training because you are using the muscles on both sides of your body, causing your brain to use both hemispheres. And while you are working your whole brain, you have the added benefit of being outside and strengthening your physical leadership too.

Taking an online course, getting an additional degree, learning a new skill, or even doing mental agility exercises such as sudoku or using the mental game app Lumosity all help to maintain your current levels. Like a muscle, your brain will atrophy if you are not pushing it. The Brain Center has learned that we can actually increase our brain functioning by learning a foreign language or a new musical instrument. These activities actually push your brain to a level where you are creating new paths in your brain. Science has proven that these exercises will actually improve mental performance with practice.

If you've established your foundation of physical fitness, including good fuel, exercise, and sleep, it will positively impact your brain function. Take care of these things, and you will be much more mentally sharp.

Another way to flex your mental leadership is to read. If you are not reading, you are behind the power curve. Obviously you have some desire to read because you are reading this book. But here are some interesting facts for comparison.

According to a Pew Research study in 2018, the typical American reads only four books a year. Bill Gates, on the other hand, reads an average of one book per week to increase his knowledge. Mark Cuban devotes at least three hours a day to reading. Elon Musk is a prolific reader and learned to build rockets by reading books. Over a thirty-year period, Steve Siebold interviewed some of the wealthiest people in the world. The majority of those interviewed cited reading as a central extracurricular activity. Most wealthy readers don't only read for entertainment, choosing education 90 percent of the time. They understand that they can only experience so much in the limited time they have in life, so in order to build mental leadership, they read so they can learn from the experiences of others. In the great words of my friend and multimillionaire Bedros Keuilian, this is called time collapsing: achieving a desired result in a reduced amount of time by leveraging your time and resources.

As with everything we discuss in this book, it starts with you. Understand what makes you tick and how you can learn more about your own challenges. The wealthiest individuals know someone else has likely faced what they are going through. They tap into that knowledge when negative conditions arise. So should you.

Sun Tzu wrote in *The Art of War*, "If you know the enemy and know yourself, you need not fear the result of a hundred battles." Use books to find those strengths and weaknesses, asking, "How can I maximize my strengths?" as you read. If you think you don't have time to get a mental edge, you're not planning to be successful. You're just making excuses for your failures.

Another way to mentally build your mind muscles is to build your Overcome Mind-Set, and the Overcome Mind-Set is built when we are pushing ourselves and uncomfortable. The great thing about learning new things is it almost always pushes us out of our comfort zones. I used to be stubborn about learning new things. Friends would say there's the easy way, the hard way, and Jay Redman's way. I will admit I am a super-slow learner and I have to learn by doing. So if you teach me something, but I don't implement it, I haven't learned it. The more we learn from people who have been through crisis or adversity, the better. This is mental leadership, and when our own catastrophe hits, we will have a toolbox of others' experiences to help us manage our own.

Obviously, learning takes time and effort. You have to create the structure to make the time and have the discipline to learn and implement new things. You've got to commit to trying to digest new concepts. Sometimes you may not agree with the concept, but maybe you can learn from it by taking the time and becoming a little uncomfortable listening to it. Who knows? It may spark an idea about how you could handle the situation better based on your personality or circumstances.

It's time to build those mental muscles and create that strong foundation in the Pentagon of Peak Performance. Take a class. Learn a language. Pick up a musical instrument. Get outside your comfort zone. Listen to leadership podcasts, journal, self-reflect. There are so many ways to train yourself mentally. Choose one and get to work.

EMOTIONAL LEADERSHIP

I WANT TO LET YOU IN ON A LITTLE SECRET. JASON "OVERCOME" Redman can be an emotional train wreck. That's right. The Overcome guy. The Navy SEAL. Even I struggle with my emotional leadership. I am naturally negative in my thinking and I run hot, so it doesn't take much to get me fired up. The great news is that when I'm aware of my emotions, I can control them, and so can you!

YOU ARE IN CONTROL!

What we do with our emotions is a choice. We choose to allow ourselves to get angry and explode. We choose to verbally express our negative thoughts and frustration. As I grew in leadership, I came to understand that a leader must always be in control of his emotions. I want to be an icon of positivity, leadership, and the Overcome Mind-Set, but to do that, I must project those things at all times.

Controlling our emotions begins by understanding the scope of our emotions and what patterns we typically fall into when we react. When I was younger, I used to wear my emotions on my sleeve. When I was excited, I bounced off the walls like a pinball in an arcade machine. When upset, I sulked. When I felt threatened, I vented my anger on anyone in my path. Every criticism was a direct attack, and I let it show. You never needed to ask where I stood, because you only had to watch me for about thirty seconds to know my mood.

It damaged my credibility as a leader and negatively impacted my relationships. I often blamed it on other people, circumstances, or bad luck, when in truth, I was solely responsible.

Pay attention to when you experience those peaks and valleys of emotion. What is triggering them? Are you fatigued? Hungry? Overwhelmed?

I know when I'm going through hard times, I can internalize the way I'm feeling and get grumpy. The emotions can be so strong that I don't think about the long-term effects of my emotional outbursts at home or work. But a single outburst can damage a relationship long-term, because it erodes trust. Think back to the last time you lost your temper or said things in an emotional outburst that you later regretted. What happened leading up to it?

A man who can't or won't control his emotions will never be able to lead others. Emotional leadership is so critical to everything we do: how we manage our emotions, how we manage negative thoughts, and how we project positivity and optimism to people around us. And the longer you work on mastering emotional leadership and projecting positivity and optimism, the more it becomes a habit.

When I talk to people about building emotional leadership, I tell them that the first step is to stop yourself from saying things that you know will create conflict. I see this all the time in relationships. Husbands and wives who needle each other. Business partners who agitate each other. I'm not talking about honest exchanges that have the family's or company's best interests at heart. I'm talking about those digs that are an emotional reaction because you're hurt, defensive, or angry. When I was in my first platoon as an officer, I was making all kinds of bad leadership decisions, but one of the biggest was my lack of emotional leadership. I was frustrated with my officer in charge.

I was frustrated with my lack of responsibility (that I deserved because of other bad decisions I was making), and I was outwardly hostile with my senior chief due to our toxic relationship. As our platoon moved through training and even into combat in Afghanistan, we would openly attack each other in front of the platoon and other units. It was toxic and a terrible example of emotional leadership. Regardless of what he said and my level of anger and frustration, I was the leader, and it was my job to set the example and stay positive. Back then, unfortunately, I was doing exactly the opposite. One of my best master chiefs gave me fantastic advice: "As a leader, never allow your personal feelings to get in the way of your professional relationships." I watch so many people do this, getting into pointless childish arguments that do nothing for them other than pull them into a negative mind-set and waste time.

If you're struggling to make those positive changes in your close relationships, start by just managing your emotions in public. Say something positive to someone you don't know, even if you don't feel like it. Smile. When the barista messes up your order for the third time, remind yourself that it's just coffee and not worth losing your cool over. If no one is shooting at you and no one is dying, you should be totally in control of your emotions. And if you are ready for the advanced level of emotional leadership, you will control your emotions even in the most dangerous situations. The most important aspect of emotional leadership is to own all decisions.

It changes your mind-set to stop believing other people can set you off, and to turn from the automatic negative thoughts that often surface during frustration. Take a few deep breaths, check yourself, and then respond in a way that shows you are in full control of yourself.

Emotional leadership is the hardest area of the pentagon for me, and the one I have to put the most effort into. I have to remember that it is a journey, not a destination. I still mess up. Last year, when our nonprofit was on the down slope with funding and our expenses were outrunning our revenues, I was preparing for our Overcome Academy class 002. After I had worked for days on the curriculum, my computer crashed. Despite my frequent saving, when I rebooted the computer, I couldn't find the document. As my level of tension, frustration, and anger began to bubble up, I should have stopped, taken a breath, and walked away for a few moments. I know myself. I know the signs when I am getting ready to boil over. But I ignored them. After twenty minutes of frantically searching, I could not find my 120-page curriculum. I slammed my computer down on my desk and screamed out a tirade of expletives. I stepped forward and promptly punched a hole in my door at exactly the same moment my bookkeeper walked toward my office to ask a question. I saw the shocked and scared look on her face, and reality set in. I was ashamed. I had lost control. I was not the leader I aspired to be in that moment, and I knew I had damaged my credibility. My IT manager later found the files buried in some weird location in my computer due to some strange error. I pulled my staff together the next day and apologized for my conduct that was unbecoming of a leader. It did not totally undo the damage from my temper tantrum, but it was a step in the right direction. I then found a meme online about controlling your emotions and taped it over the hole on my door as a humorous reminder to my staff and myself that I would be better.

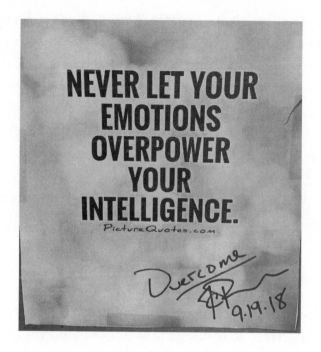

Remember, we are not perfect. We will mess up. The difference between peak performers and others is that peak performers seek to constantly change and get better, and average people settle and accept that "this is just the way I am."

The last thing I will say about emotional leadership is about controlling your input. If you do nothing but scroll on social media wishing you were someone else, watch inflammatory news pundits, and hang out with negative people in places where you tend to get emotional, you are not taking emotional leadership of your life. I no longer watch the news. I only use social media to advance my message of positivity, self-leadership, and the Over-come Mind-Set. If I follow you, it is because I know beyond a shadow of doubt you are a positive person. If you suddenly start down a road of negativity, I unfollow you. You have to do the same in your life. You want to be positive and have more success? Remove yourself from places and spaces where you know you are not in emotional control. Plan ahead and visualize a different positive outcome, whether that means taking that deep breath and walking away calmly, or finding the right words to say, like, "Let me get back to you on that." Whatever your response, prepare it ahead of time and get serious about taking control of your emotions.

SOCIAL LEADERSHIP

SOCIAL LEADERSHIP IS HOW WE SELECT AND INVEST IN OUR FAMILIES, friendships, and teams. Social leadership is a well-managed set of four rings. The smallest, closest ring of influence is your immediate family. The next ring includes close friends and extended family. The third ring holds work relationships and acquaintances. The outermost ring is any other external influence: the barista at our favorite coffee shop, people we meet at a conference, old high school or college friends that we don't keep in touch with.

Many people focus so much on their work relationships that they ignore or neglect their innermost circles. I have to tell you, when life ambushes happen, when you find yourself on the X, it is not the external work relationships that are going to make a difference. Some of those people will be there for you, and that's great, but it's going to be the internal relationships—your friends and family—that will help you get off the X. You have to take the time to build those relationships, because in those most critical moments, it is our most important teammates, those inner circles, that are going to help us get off the X.

When I got myself in trouble, my social leadership was lacking. I had damaged my work relationships, and my acquaintances disappeared. Often in those hardest moments you only have your close friends and family, and if you did not take the time to nourish those relationships, you will be trying to overcome the near impossible, climbing out of a deep hole without a rope or assistance.

Thankfully, when that enemy ambush happened, my social leadership was rock solid. My teammates were there for me. I had an amazing wife who was by far the best nurse that I could have had. I had three beautiful children who showed me the definition of unconditional love. Their love got me out of bed every single morning, and it made me say, "I don't care how bad I'm messed up, I'm going to drive forward."

Build your circles of influence! I was ready because my social leadership, my network, and my teams were strong. If you have people that are pulling you down, get rid of them, because in the hardest moments, when you're on the X, they're not going to help you get off of it. Social leadership means taking stock of who you surround yourself with daily, and making sure you prioritize relationships. It is critical to choose the rings of influence around us wisely, both personally and professionally.

I recently talked to retired general Stan McChrystal about the ambush that happened to him in 2010 that led to his resignation after a thirty-four-year military career. Most people saw the unflattering *Rolling Stone* story about his command team. It caused a big dustup, and he offered his resignation to President Barack Obama, who accepted it. McChrystal explained, "To a degree, I can argue to myself that the article was inaccurate and focused on a specific agenda, but ultimately it doesn't matter. It landed on the president's desk and he shouldn't have to deal with negative stories coming out of one of the military commanders. I accepted responsibility and don't have any regrets."

The life ambush was completely unexpected. McChrystal always knew the battlefield was a dangerous place, that he could be injured, killed, lose comrades, be fired for incompetence—but this? This was so entirely outside what he had imagined possible. His first response was disbelief, sincerely hoping he would wake up from this unbelievable turn of events.

He had a range of responses from his social circles. There were those who distanced themselves. There were those who were no longer in proximity because he'd given up his job. There were those who said, "You're getting screwed. This isn't fair." It was tempting to listen to those voices and agree. They had good intentions in their support of him.

But ultimately, it was his wife, his most important teammate and inner ring of his social leadership, who showed him the way off the X. She said, "It doesn't matter how it happened. It happened. Now we move forward. Period. Don't stay back there." McChrystal said her unwavering support helped them decide together not to get stuck in the past. He couldn't do anything to change the past.

McChrystal's investment in time with his inner ring of social leadership—his wife and family—made a huge difference for him in a major life ambush. Even with the amazing support of his wife, leaving the world he'd spent his whole adult life serving was incredibly difficult. It shook his emotional confidence, and he said at times he felt like damaged goods. As he moved in their social circles, people were nice out of sympathy, but he noticed that it felt like the warmth of respect and genuine affection was often lacking. He remembers walking through airports those first few months, feeling like there was a spotlight on him, since he had been on television every day. He felt the eyes, the questions. He admitted that it was embarrassing. He knew some people were whispering hateful things, untrue things, negative things. It was easy to think everyone saw him in a negative light.

But then, someone would lean over and extend a hand, looking him in the eye, whether it was the TSA agent checking his identification or a seatmate on the plane.

"You're General McChrystal? Thank you for your service."

So many people create negative stories and assumptions in their minds when something goes horribly awry in life, and they have a natural tendency to push people away in their crisis. The vast majority of the time these negative assumptions are wrong, and with a little communication and a refusal to push away the world, we can maintain our solid level of social leadership.

As McChrystal continued to travel and move forward with his life, he realized that most of the interactions were positive. People moved on to the next news story quickly. They had their own lives and concerns. Because of his wife's social leadership and his own resolve to continue to put himself out there in public, in both social and professional circles, he overcame an incident that could have easily kept him out of the public eye for the rest of his life.

He explained, "The world moves on. It's only a problem when you don't. You can live in it and walk as a living reminder of the trouble you've experienced, or you can keep moving and let your new actions show your true leadership. Revenge, retribution is pointless—they're a waste of time and energy you can spend on other things. It's a lot better to say, 'It happened, and I'm moving on.' And if you have a sense of humor, you might even be able to say, good for them, they got me. They did a good job."

The last component of social leadership is communicating with those around us. Because we live in our own world day in and day out, we automatically assume people know where we are going or what we are going through. They don't. We have to communicate our intentions. Just like McChrystal and his wife communicated clearly about their direction and values, you have to choose communication and engagement over isolation. After an ambush, you often feel alone. You don't necessarily want to communicate with others, but it is essential to have a team you trust around you.

Communicate and engage with your family by taking a genuine interest in what your spouse and kids are doing. Meet with friends and tend to those positive relationships.

In business, surround yourself with people who are positive, who are moving in the same direction as you.

If you struggle with small talk like I do, make that a place where you move into the zone of discomfort. Think ahead and prepare a few questions that will work for the people you'll be with, and then follow through. Of course, you'll have some awkward moments, but keep pushing through and you will grow.

There are no shortcuts to strong social leadership, because

relationships take time and effort. It's worth it, though. Those relationships are what make life worthwhile.

SPIRITUAL LEADERSHIP

SPIRITUAL LEADERSHIP IS AT THE HIGHEST LEVEL OF THE PENTAGON of Peak Performance. Most people ignore completely or struggle with spiritual leadership. Spiritual leadership means recognizing that you are a unique part of a much larger world and picture, and investing time and resources to make your community and world better. Spiritual leadership can mean mindfulness, meditation, mentorship, philanthropy, religion, or a combination of all of these.

The foundation of spiritual leadership is perspective—understanding that the world is much bigger than you, and, if you live in America, that the majority of your problems pale in comparison to those of so many who live in extreme poverty or war-torn countries around the globe. As I have traveled the world, I have seen the absolute best and worst humankind has to offer. I have had the great privilege of riding at times in private jets with multimillionaires, experiencing the highest levels of opulence, and I have seen the unequivocal lowest levels of poverty on this planet. I have witnessed some of the most vile displays of depravity that you could ever comprehend, things that would make you ask, "How could a human being do this to another human being?" These experiences give me perspective. Perspective is how we look at the world and how we allow the things that occur around us to shape our decision making and our actions.

I meet people all the time who have a negative outlook and a negative mind-set. I hear one phrase above all others that drives me insane and tells me in a split second that this individual has poor perspective. Something will go wrong, and as the person grows more and more agitated, more and more anxious, the stress bubbles up. They will almost always say, "Oh my God, what a bad day." I'm willing to bet there's someone reading this right now who has said that today.

Most people confuse a bad day with a schedule disruption or an inconvenience. Your day didn't turn out the way you thought it was going to. You were not able to follow the schedule you had laid out for yourself, and you allow these disruptions to twist your perspective into negativity. Spiritual leadership enables us to step outside of ourselves in these hard or frustrating moments. To pause, be grateful, and appreciate that this minor inconvenience pales in comparison to the bad days of millions of other people on this planet.

For me, spiritual leadership means a strong faith in God, meeting with other people who share my beliefs, and living for more than myself. My faith journey had been reignited in Iraq. That night when I called out to God in the middle of that firefight and I had that sudden influx of energy, enabling me to get up and walk off the battlefield, I felt like God had given me a second chance at life, and I wanted to make the most of it. Your spiritual leadership might look different, but it is worth investing in the understanding that there is a much bigger world that you can impact than just the small sphere you live in.

If you struggle with spiritual leadership, try a simple practice: gratitude. Write down three things you are grateful for each night for thirty days. It will change your outlook. Gratitude forces you to look outside of yourself, to focus on something beyond your problems. One of my mentors, Bedros Keuilian, actually texts three different people he's grateful for each day in his life.

A second practice that will spiritually enrich your life is generosity. Give of your time and resources each week. Sharing your talents or the lessons you've learned helps both you and your audience. There's real power in being able to make connections through honest generosity.

Other ways to build spiritual leadership include everything from taking a walk in nature to attending a yoga or meditation class. You could try a sensory deprivation tank, or volunteer in your community. All of these activities force you to focus on something besides yourself and your problems.

Mark Divine uses Zen meditation to guide his spiritual practice. Meditation changed his life and guides all his decisions now. He gave several great tips for what this might look like for you:

1. Practice deep silence and introspection. For this, you must be able to silence your mind and turn that mental flashlight inward to begin to see what makes you tick.
2. Use your crisis to refine what you believe about yourself and the world around you. When you have a serious crisis, you are a different person. Ego dies and you awaken to a much more spiritual view of humanity, who you are, and what you are going to do about it. You leave the crisis much more grounded if you allow yourself to take the time to consider the deeper spiritual lessons.

3. Open yourself to others. Mother Teresa didn't meditate; she served her fellow human beings with a radically open heart that produced the same state as meditation.

Whatever spirituality looks like for you, build that perspective. Be grateful and recognize that you have the ability to make a difference by giving back your time, talents, and resources. Take the time weekly to connect with something larger than yourself. It will have tremendous long-lasting benefits for your health and recovery, and enable you to better appreciate everything else around you.

YOU WILL BE READY

FIVE LEGS. HOW MANY OF YOUR LEGS ARE WOBBLY? HOW MANY aren't even attached anymore? After reading this, do you feel like a brisk wind could blow your table over?

The reality is that you have the potential to live a great life. There are amazing things in your future. But there are also things that will conspire to destroy you, to overpower you with overwhelming force. And as I said at the beginning of the chapter, if you're *not* in a life ambush right now, there's a good chance one is out there waiting for you.

You have the ability to choose *right now* if you're going to be prepared. Now is the time to build yourself in all five areas of the pentagon so you *will* be ready to face any challenge and overcome.

One leg? Your table can't stand. Two legs? It'll fall over just as fast. Three legs? The table can stand up, but you wouldn't want to push it too hard. Four legs? That's a solid table. It would take a good effort to turn it over. Five legs though? Good luck pushing over that table.

How many legs are you going to have on your table? How strong is your pentagon going to be? Now is the time to choose.

Ready to Build Your Strong Pentagon?

Go to www.getoffx.com and get my **72 Hours to Peak Performance** online course.

CHAPTER 8

ADAPT TO THE UNEXPECTED

The only thing that makes life unfair is the delusion that it should be fair.

—Steve Maraboli

WHEN ADMIRAL ERIC OLSON BEGAN HIS CAREER AT THE US NAVAL Academy in Annapolis, he found he wasn't interested in running the highly technical mass maneuvers on big deck ships that make up a rising officer's role. One Friday night at dinner, he heard an announcement that would change the course of his career and life:

"Anyone who wants to be a SEAL should show up in room 110 after dinner."

At that time, the SEAL teams had only been in existence for ten years or so, and there was little information available outside of whispers and legends. It was Olson's final year at the academy, and along with fifty or so other midshipmen, he went to the meeting only to find himself being berated by the SEAL lieutenant who barked out sharp criticism, explaining how none of them would be qualified to be SEALs, they weren't worthy, they were too weak, and they probably didn't have the fortitude to last even one day. After verbally abusing the room for fifteen minutes, the SEAL closed with an invitation: "If you think you have what it takes to give it a shot, show up on Monday afternoon for a screening test."

Monday afternoon, twenty-five midshipmen, including Olson, showed up for the physical screening test. There they were ranked from one to twenty-five. The top fifteen were invited for interviews. Finally, only three were selected to go to BUD/S after graduation.

Olson was one of them.

The whole selection process was complete by Tuesday: from the announcement Friday night to the screening and interviews on Monday and Tuesday. Done. He'd changed the course of his Navy career in five days. He had a new mission: become a Navy SEAL. He would graduate in May and be at BUD/S by October. His future was falling into place.

Three days later, Olson's Volkswagen van careened into a guardrail at sixty miles per hour. The van flipped twice and stopped with Olson's head trapped beneath it. He was unconscious for hours before someone with a jack was able to lift the van off of him and get him to the emergency room.

Portions of his scalp and face had collapsed, and he had lost teeth, ruptured his colon, broken his femur, and nearly severed an Achilles tendon.

Olson was in intensive care for ten days before he was wheeled in bed up to the ward where he would continue recovery for the next two months, most of it in traction for his broken femur.

"That's too bad—I heard you were going to be a SEAL," the nurse said, patting his arm.

Six months from graduation, less than eleven months from his BUD/S assignment, and now Olson's entire future was as busted as his leg. After nearly four years in the Naval Academy, he had finally found his calling, only to have it ripped away from him just as fast.

What was he going to do now? How could he adapt to *this*? Was there any chance he could still complete his mission and achieve his dream of becoming a SEAL?

IT'S NOT FAIR

EVERYTHING IN SEAL TRAINING IS BUILT ON ADAPTING TO THE unexpected. If you come in thinking life is fair, SEAL training will beat it out of you. So many that have never been through BUD/S talk about how physically grueling it is. They are absolutely correct. But those of us that have been through it know that it is 10 percent physical and 90 percent mental. And the reason it's 90 percent mental is because SEAL training is designed to screw with your head.

All through training, the instructors will tell you exactly how to do things, and then when you do them precisely the right way, they will tell you you failed. It's outrageously unfair.

"Complete this task on this timeline."

You do it on that timeline. Then they fail you.

"Drop and give me fifty."

As students, we used to jokingly call it "BUD/S Time," a distortion of the space-time continuum.

If you end up failing to complete an evolution on time, it isn't uncommon to hear, "Obviously, on the last evolution, we did not give you enough time. We told you to do it in thirty seconds. So *now* you're going to do it in twenty-five seconds. *Go!*"

You play this game for hours, days, weeks.

The guys who can't accept the arbitrary rules, the guys who think that at some point they're actually going to get it right, usually quit first. They just can't wrap their heads around the fact that it will always be unfair because it's designed that way on purpose.

Guess what? Life is unfair, and combat is unequivocally unfair.

Crazy things happen in combat that you don't expect and can't plan for. A bomb could blow up, killing everyone around you, while you escape without a scratch. The best soldier in a platoon could be wounded in action, while the worst goes unscathed. There's no rhyme or reason.

SEAL instructors want to prepare you for that from day one, and in training, they're looking for individuals who can deal with heavy doses of bone-crushing, unfair punishment and still drive forward to get things done. Even something as simple as a room inspection is an opportunity to learn "fairness," or the lack thereof.

Before room inspection, the instructors will tell you exactly how your room needs to be cleaned. It's not rocket science. You clean your room perfectly. When the room inspection begins, you stand at attention listening to the chaos move through the building. As the instructors approach your room, you hear curses and shouting as each room fails.

Not me, you think. *My room is perfect.*

When they finally step into your room, you begin to sweat as you watch students run by your room dripping in sand and salt water after they failed and got their punishment on the beach.

On one room inspection, my squadmates and I knew we had achieved perfection. When the instructors entered our room, they walked around and talked about how perfect the room was.

"THIS is the cleanest room I have ever seen," one instructor said.

Another nodded. "We should have the rest of the class come in here and see how it is done. This is the level everyone should be working to achieve."

"It's a triumph," the first instructor said, checking the final corner.

At nineteen years old, I actually believed them.

The instructor in the corner stepped to the middle of the room, frowning. "You know what's wrong with this room?" He pointed to a spot on the floor. We looked to where he pointed like a bunch of dummies, staring at a gleaming, shining floor that Mr. Clean himself would have been proud of. Suddenly, the senior chief instructor pulled a handful of sand out of his pocket and dropped it on the floor.

"There's sand on the floor," he said. "Fail!"

We ran to the beach with the rest of the unit.

This is bullshit, I thought. *They cheated!*

I didn't get the lesson they were teaching until years later. No matter how perfect your preparation, you can still be wrong and fail in an absolutely catastrophic and unexpected way.

The key isn't to avoid failure. That's impossible. The key lies in how you get past that failure and how quickly you motivate and inspire the people around you to drive forward.

In an unfair world, you have to adapt. You have to OVERCOME.

In that hospital, Eric Olson hadn't yet learned the lessons from BUD/S. Would he be able to get past the absolute unfairness of his injuries? How could he recover physically and finish school to keep his dream alive?

VISUALIZE ALL OUTCOMES

ONE KEY COMPONENT OF ADAPTATION IS THINKING THROUGH WHAT might happen. If you can visualize possible outcomes, you can plan to mitigate the effects of those worst-case scenarios. Secretary of Defense Robert Gates wanted to be proactive in how we managed our casualties and medevac flow in the Iraq War. There is a "golden hour" of trauma care, meaning that if an individual can survive the first hour and get emergency care, their chances of survival increase exponentially. Bob Gates pushed for a nightly analysis of missions going on in the combat theater and then strategically placed helicopter refueling areas, or FARPs (Forward Arming and Refueling Points), so that if there were injuries due to a battle, the helicopters were situated across the battlefield to cover as much area as possible in the least amount of time. As a result, the majority of casualties during that period received emergency care within the golden hour. I am alive today because a leader and his team visualized all outcomes and prepared for contingencies.

In the SEAL teams, every team member brainstorms the scenarios, plans contingencies, and talks about the absolute worst-case scenarios. Then we train to deal with as many as possible. We might not see any of the scenarios we create, but the exercise teaches us to adapt to changing conditions. The practice runs show us a variety of ways to meet those challenges, and if we do encounter something similar on the battlefield, we are not trying to come up with solutions in a crisis situation when time is of the essence.

I remember going after a high-level Al Qaeda financier on one mission in Iraq. As we discussed the upcoming mission, we evaluated the different courses of action and contingency plans on how my team would approach the target building from a larger open ground area than the other assault teams. We discussed what would happen if heavy weapons opened up on us from the house as we moved across hundreds of yards of open terrain. We noticed in our pictures that there were sewage ditches roughly every fifty yards that ran across the open terrain. We knew if heavy gunfire erupted, we only had to move roughly twenty-five yards forward or backward and into one of those sewage ditches to get cover from the withering fire. I definitely remember that contingency plan because I thought to myself, *Great, if we get in the shit, we have to jump into the shit to save our lives.* But if it had happened, we already had a plan for the unexpected and would have reacted.

The same principle applies in life. To adapt and overcome, you have to think ahead, pay attention to signs, and plan for the worst.

When the doctor tells you, "Man, if you don't make a change

to your diet and exercise, you are putting yourself at risk," you owe it to yourself, at least for a few minutes, to ask, "If I continue to avoid dealing with this problem, what's the worst-case scenario?" You could have a heart attack or a stroke. Ask your doctor for the worst-case scenario if you can't identify it for yourself. It's better to have straight answers than to rely on guesswork.

Once you know the worst-case scenario, be proactive to prevent that ambush from happening. I meet so many people who step into a life ambush and say, "Oh my God, that was so unexpected!" but when they dig into what happened to them, it turns out they had been given multiple signs beforehand but failed or procrastinated to take action. They let the ambush happen from laziness and ignorance.

NO MATTER WHAT, NO MATTER HOW

THE VERY LAST COMPONENT OF ADAPTING TO THE UNEXPECTED comes full circle to what we talked about at the opening of this chapter. It is the mind-set that's programmed into you from day one of SEAL training—the mind-set that it will always be unfair, so don't give up. No matter how well you train. No matter how well you plan. No matter how well you prepare. Expect it to be unfair, but drive forward and complete the mission.

I remember going through close quarters combat training years ago. Close quarters combat is a fancy name for clearing a building or house with guns and explosives. There are multiple tactics and strategies to do this safely, efficiently, and as quickly as possible. In this scenario we were using live role players and paint-filled bullets in our guns called Simunition. On this iteration, they had told us a specific door was off-limits, meaning to ignore it. No one was supposed to come through that door. They had put a big *X* with caution tape on the door to signify it was "out of play."

After a half day of doing iterations through the house, the instructors quietly removed the *X* from the door. As we made our next run through the house, we had been conditioned to ignore that door, but this time it was in play, and as the instructors expected, we did not cover that door. We blew right by it. As soon as we called that room secure and were moving our people past it, someone opened the door and started shooting our guys in the back.

A bad leader would say, "You told us that nobody would come in from this door over there, that it was off-limits, so we didn't check it!"

But it was our fault for not being aware that something had changed. The unexpected had happened, as it always will. SEALs do that on purpose, *always* training for the unexpected, because we want our people to constantly recognize that the unexpected can happen.

We have a saying: "Despite your best plan, the enemy always has a vote." This applies in business too. Despite your best plans, the market and your competition always have a vote. Are you ready to adapt to their unexpected actions?

In the real world, thankfully, failing to adapt doesn't usually result in immediate life or death. But a lack of reaction time can still ruin a great business deal, meeting opportunity, or significant event. Resolve to act and drive forward, no matter what, no matter how.

ADAPTATION EQUALS ACTION

ONE OF THE MOST IMPRESSIVE ADAPTATIONS I'VE SEEN RECENTLY WAS relayed to me at a speaking engagement. A young man about my age came up to me after the event, and we started talking. He told me his story of failure and overcoming. He was a senior chief petty officer in the Navy at the time. He was playing in a military nonprofit golf tournament, and he'd spent the day drinking. Hammered, he stole the golf course mowing machine and was riding around, screaming obscenities on base. The military police arrested him and charged him with drunken disorderly conduct and conduct unbecoming of a senior noncommissioned officer. He was one of the senior men at his command at the time and was getting ready to step into the number-one position for his rank. Despite the charges, he believed that given his exceptional superior performance up to that time, they would just give him a slap on the wrist and say, "Hey, that was bad. Don't let that happen again," but they didn't.

He ended up with what's called an NJP, nonjudicial punishment—an Article 15. The military uses its own legal system based on the Uniform Code of Military Justice. An Article 15 gives a commander the ability to impose punishment without having the infraction go to an official military trial. Article 15 is used for more minor offenses but still can leave a major black mark on your record. They confronted him about his behavior, and he was charged and found guilty. They reduced his rank from senior chief to chief petty officer, which also affected his pay. He was stunned, but they told him that it could be reviewed after six months, based on his behavior, and potentially reversed.

Here he was, rocking along at this high level of his career, and he had this major incident that caused him to lose his current leadership position and resulted in a reduction in rank. He'd been in the military for a long time at this point. When he was telling me this story, I expected him to regale me with a tale of spiraling down when all of this occurred, but I was pleased to hear the opposite. For him, the findings of the Article 15 became a launch point. He adapted in several ways.

The first thing he did was start asking people, "Do you think I have a drinking problem?"

People told him the truth: "Yeah, you drink too much and get out of hand when you're drunk."

He cut out alcohol, cold turkey. He took full responsibility and began working on leading himself again. He began to set a good example. He made remarkable progress and hoped that within six months, they would review his case and return his rank based on his progress. He fully believed they would see how much he'd changed and reinstate him.

When the time came to review the case, a new commanding officer had stepped in. He had a zero-tolerance mind-set against alcohol infractions and had noticed multiple alcohol-related incidents within the command. Despite the senior chief's exceptional performance before the golf course incident, and despite his exemplary behavior the last six months, the commanding officer wanted to make an example out of him that he would not tolerate alcohol-related incidents in his command.

They voted against the reinstatement. He was crushed.

After this second life ambush, I fully expected to hear that he then returned to drinking. At a certain point, without a relentless Overcome Mind-Set, people get tired of getting knocked down and don't get back up. They stay on the X, start feeling sorry for themselves and self-medicating.

"Did you start drinking again after that?" I asked him.

"No. I realized that I had caused the problem in the first place," he told me.

I was impressed. It would have been so easy to point to other cases where people had been reinstated, to scream about the unfairness, to highlight the years of solid service. He didn't wallow in those thoughts. He accepted that he'd caused his life ambush and that the reinstatement was outside his control. He adapted to his disappointment by continuing on the path he knew would lead to a better version of himself—not the same old person, but a new, wiser person who had a clear understanding of how decisions can derail a life. That's remarkable adaptation, because it was grounded fully in continued action. He refused to stay on the X. Movement is life, and he continued to adapt, drive forward, and move toward new goals.

The bottom line: Ambushes are on the horizon. Will you be ready when they come? Your ability to adapt to the unexpected is the critical component to getting off the X the fastest and starting your new journey of success.

YOUR CHOICE

"That's too bad—I heard you were going to be a seal."

When Eric Olson survived his car accident, he didn't know what the future held, but he knew he wasn't giving up that easy. He ignored his leg in traction, ignored the tubes and monitors and IV. He looked the nurse right in the eye.

"I *am* going to be a SEAL."

He must have been a sight, with his face mangled, his head still bandaged, his monitors beeping. But his dream was intact. He would have to adapt to his new conditions, but he was determined to press forward.

To her credit, she met his gaze and responded in kind.

"Then we better help you get ready."

The nurse and staff helped shift Olson's bed configuration into a mini-gym, so that while he was in traction, he could do pull-ups, dips, and curls in his hospital bed.

A few days later, she returned with a surprise. "If you're going to be a SEAL," she said, "you should probably meet one."

"Sure," he said.

She wheeled in none other than Tommy Norris. He was a legend, having taken part in rescuing two downed pilots in Vietnam (for which he was later awarded the Medal of Honor), before taking life-threatening gunfire in an intelligence-gathering mission six months later. Norris was in the hospital recovering from his injuries, and only weighed about ninety-eight pounds. Half his face was missing, he was blind in one eye, and he struggled to speak. The hero still had a considerable journey ahead toward his own recovery, but he took the time to talk to Eric Olson. They visited for a while, and at the end, Olson shook his hand.

"Lieutenant Norris, is there anything you regret about becoming a SEAL?" Olson asked.

"The only thing I regret is that they're going to prevent me from continuing to do it," he said. "I love it so much."

Olson said that meeting renewed and fueled his mission to become a SEAL. "If a guy who suffered such egregious injuries as a SEAL could still talk about it with that passion, then it was good enough for me too."

Olson continued to get stronger, and he was released from the hospital in January. His graduation was in June. Olson was so determined not to miss his shot that he talked the doctors out of casting his leg, becoming one of the first fractured-femur patients not to be casted, and he was instead put in a weight-bearing polio brace. Each day, he would take off his brace, jump in a pool, and work to strengthen his body. A couple of months later, he was able to shed the brace and run a half mile. He never wavered from his mission.

In October, he went to BUD/S. He realized that with all his focus to strengthen his leg, he'd neglected his upper body, and he fell from the top of the Slide for Life twice during the same obstacle course, landed on his back twenty-five feet below, and garnered probation the first few weeks of BUD/S while he strengthened his upper body. Nevertheless, he worked through his probation and made it through BUD/S on his first try. He graduated as the honor man of his class, which turned out to be the smallest class in the history of BUD/S. Out of fifty-four men, Olson stood as one of just four to make it through.

At every turn, Admiral Olson met unexpected obstacles. From the accident and broken femur to being on probation during BUD/S, he overcame by adapting to the conditions and relying on his commitment to his mission to become a SEAL. He did not deviate from that path, and he served for thirty-seven years before retiring in 2011, adapting to the unexpected every step of the way.

Life isn't fair. If you think it will go easy on you, think again.

Just because you've found some success at some point in your life, it doesn't mean you can coast on your achievements. No, success only guarantees that more hardship is headed your way.

The good news is that you are tough enough to deal with it. You *can* overcome. Just as Admiral Olson did, you can look the obstacle in the face and say, "I don't know how, but I *am* going to accomplish my mission. It means too much to me to give up now."

That doesn't mean you can do it alone. Just as Olson wouldn't have accomplished his mission without the help of the nurse who helped him train, the doctors who helped repair his body and then allowed him to not wear a cast, and the inspiration of Tommy Norris, you won't be able to accomplish your mission without the help and support of the people around you.

But no one can support you unless you give them something to support. It begins with you. When life treats you unfairly, are you going to give in and let the world have its way? Or are you going to adapt? Are you going to shift tactics, try something new, get some help, and then launch afresh?

Are you going to overcome?

PART 2 DEBRIEF

- Your life mission is your larger purpose and passion. Clarify it.
- Change is never comfortable. Stop expecting it to be easy and embrace the zone of discomfort to create lasting change in your life.
- If you don't invest the time and self-discipline to strengthen all five sides of your Pentagon of Peak Performance, you're not going to be ready for an ambush. Get proactive.
- Use your Overcome Mind-Set to get past the belief that life should be fair. It isn't, and you'll have to adapt to the unexpected to keep pushing forward toward your life mission.

IMMEDIATE ACTION DRILL: REACT

Part 2 is about the self-discipline and Overcome Mind-Set that make you ready to face anything thrown at you in business or life. Take a few minutes to REACT.

- **Recognize your reality:** Take stock of your current physical, mental, emotional, social, and spiritual condition. Get honest and stop minimizing the risks you're taking.
- **Evaluate your position:** Which leg of your Pentagon of Peak Performance is weakest? Evaluate the key factors influencing your current state: list the things you ARE doing that are harmful as well as the things you're NOT doing that would make you stronger.
- **Assess possible exit routes:** For one or two legs of the Pentagon, write down all the ways you could address that area of your life. If you think you're in crisis in all five areas, then begin with physical and get to a doctor to assess your risks.
- **Choose a direction and communicate it:** You won't stick with forty changes made all at once, so choose one or two from your list and go full throttle on those. You can always add the next change from your list once you've made progress. Tell someone you trust about your course of action and ask them to hold you accountable.
- **Take action:** DO IT. Not tomorrow, not next week, not when you get a little more cash in the bank. Do it now.

Remember that you have the Overcome Mind-Set to push through when you want to quit. No quitting! You are taking control of your life again through self-discipline, and you are much stronger than your mind is going to let you believe. As you take action, write down your progress!

PART 3

LEAD OTHERS

CHAPTER 9

GET YOUR HEAD UNDER THE BOAT

Alone we can do so little; together we can do so much.

—Helen Keller

COMPANIES HIRE ME TO SPEAK ALL OVER THE COUNTRY, AND OFTEN one of their leaders will approach me and say, "You were a Navy SEAL leader. Help me lead my team better." I always have the same answer:

"How well do you lead yourself?"

If they ignore my question or say, "No, you misunderstood; I'm asking how I can lead *my people* better," I know they've missed the point. So many people confuse leadership with telling people what to do. They fail to realize leading people has less to do with the words that come out of their mouth and more to do with their actions leading up to that moment. If you skip the Pentagon of Peak Performance and self-discipline, you're undermining your ability to lead others. There's no way around it. Every part of leading others stems from your own core of resilience, the positive attitude you project, and the example you set. That self-discipline and positivity will help you lead after an ambush. If you watch effective leaders, they might make it look easy, but I guarantee they've put in the time and self-discipline that make others want to follow.

As a leader navigating crisis in your business or family, you have one job: get your team in motion toward a shared mission. I see it time and again. Leaders who suffer an ambush react by disengaging or by charging ahead alone. Neither option will inspire others to follow you, and in the words of Vince Peterson, the man who talked me out of quitting Ranger School and torching my military career, "People will follow you if you give them a reason to." One of the best ways to start that journey back to leadership is to reengage your mission alongside your people. In BUD/S training, we call this "getting your head under the boat."

During BUD/S training, we work with small rubber boats called IBSs (inflatable boat smalls) in seven-man teams. You and your team run around the base with the 250-pound boat on top of your head. As you haul the boat in and out of the surf, it gets heavier as water and sand accumulate. Every now and then an instructor will crawl up in your boat, and you get an extra 200 pounds to carry around. Even without an instructor on board, carrying that boat hurts. It hurts your head; it hurts your neck. As you run, the boats bounce, rubbing off patches of your hair by the end of training. If you go out and watch a class in training, you'll hear one cry above all others as the students run by carrying the boats on top of their heads:

"Get your head under the boat!"

You hear it over and over because a member of the boat crew will, for a moment, try to relieve the pressure on his head by moving out from underneath the boat for a brief respite.

But as soon as he does that, it transfers the weight. His seventh of the weight suddenly redistributes across everybody else. More specifically, the brunt of the weight transfers to the opposite side. If he's in the back left position, the front right position suddenly feels the bulk of that weight. The guy who disengages feels a moment of relief, but it's always at the expense of another member of the boat crew. Every single man on the team feels that shift in responsibility, and while they all understand why someone would seek that relief, they immediately demand he return to his responsibilities with the phrase, "Get your head under the boat!"

It's such a clear illustration of teamwork and the necessity of each individual's effort. The team is communicating, "We need you to carry your weight. You're not helping out." In boat teams, when you take a break, not only are you slacking off, but you're forcing other people to carry your weight. It impedes the team and creates animosity. It incites anger. It makes you less efficient. The rest of the team is tired because they're carrying your weight. When you're tired or uncomfortable, if you take a break while nobody else is, you just screw over everybody around you and make things worse.

As a team, we need to operate in unison until we decide there's a breaking point or until we get to the end. You've got to keep your head under the boat at all times. Even the leader has to have his head under the boat, right there with the team, motivating and inspiring them to finish strong together.

COMMITMENT TO COORDINATED MOVEMENT

NO MATTER WHAT'S ON THE SCHEDULE, WHENEVER THE SURF IS BIG, everything gets cleared for surf passage in the boats. Successful surf passage requires you to operate as a unified team. Every single task related to the boat requires teamwork and synchronization, from something that seems simple, like picking the boat up and getting it on top of your head, to the more complex task of rowing the boat through the surf.

The boat teams who are most successful develop a rhythm, a cadence, and a clear designation of what is expected by each member and when. To be successful, everybody has to be rowing in the same direction. On broken teams, one or more people are focused on themselves instead of trying to move in the direction where the team should be going.

When you're out in the surf zone and you're trying to row through the giant waves, everyone must row at exactly the same time. The boat crew leader gives commands—"Stroke! Stroke!"—and everybody needs to be digging their paddle in and stroking at the same time. When you go up into the face of a ten-, twelve-, or fifteen-foot wave, you can easily be turned over if everyone isn't giving it their all. This is especially true if one side of the boat digs their paddles in at a different time than the other side of the boat, which will cause the boat to turn abruptly. Then, the boat is canted in the face of the wave, and a crash is coming. The only way to go through the top of a large wave is straight and fast, to break through the lip and get on the other side. If you're canted or at an angle, it flips you over and smashes you. It's critical to row in the same direction at the same time to avoid that flip.

In early surf passage evolutions, you get smashed all the time. The instructors don't tell you what to expect. There are no "top tips and hacks for surf passage!" pamphlets. They want you to learn in the crucible of training. Failure and hardship are effective instructors. Everyone in that boat might want to be a leader, and they may have great leadership abilities, but in the moment, all that matters is that they are an effective member of the team, able to take commands and follow them for the benefit of all.

The boat crew leader is the coxswain. He has his paddle in the water behind the boat as a rudder, and it's his job to keep the boat as straight as possible from the back, where he coordinates the cadence. He communicates the position and the direction through his clear commands. His final role is that of motivator— his encouragement keeps the crew in motion and paddling, even when the surf threatens to flip them. Without a strong boat crew leader, the boat will likely flip. Without strong team members, the boat's dead in the water. It takes coordinated movement and cooperation by all.

As you lead your team after an ambush, remember that image of a boat crew moving in a coordinated effort toward the goal. You lead by example when you are working alongside your team, directing and motivating not because you are in charge, but because you are in the boat together chasing a common mission.

CLEAR ROLES: MAIN EFFORT VERSUS SUPPORT

ONE OF THE MOST IMPORTANT PARTS OF COORDINATED MOVEMENT is a clear delineation of roles. In the Army, they talk about the main effort versus supporting effort. The main effort is the overall strategic objective or mission. In Iraq, for example, the main effort was to secure the city of Baghdad. The supporting efforts were all the micro missions that had to be done in order to accomplish the main mission.

Let's use a sports analogy. In professional football, the main effort is to win. The supporting efforts are the offense, defense, special teams, coaches, trainers, recruiters, and even administrative support personnel. The supporting efforts can be even more specific "departments" within each of the aforementioned, such as the quarterback team on the offense or the linebacker team on the defense. Each one of them has to understand their specific role in accomplishing the main effort.

Businesses have the same separation of roles. In a nonprofit supporting wounded warriors, the main effort is the actual direct work with our warriors. The supporting effort includes the different components that make that work possible, from scheduling to marketing, to fundraising, to event management, to case management, to accounting, to sponsor/donor relations, and more. All the different parts work together to make the main effort successful in accomplishing the overarching mission.

Teams and organizations who fail to keep their support efforts in tune with the main effort, or who let silos develop within the team or organization, are headed for trouble. The entire team has to be focused on their role in accomplishing the mission. When there are miscommunications or supporting efforts out of alignment with the main effort, it's a leadership failure. They've lost sight of where they're headed and are off course. An organization with misaligned supporting efforts may be able to continue to function for a time, but the longer you wait to address problems, the less likely you are to accomplish the main effort effectively. No one coaches a sports team to lose games or leads a business to lose money intentionally, but if you don't keep people focused on the main effort, that is exactly what you are doing.

When I was in treatment after my combat injuries, various teams of doctors and specialists owned different pieces of real estate on my body. I had an orthopedics team, a general surgery team, an oral maxillofacial team, a plastic surgery team, an eye doctor, and an ear, nose, and throat team. I even had an infectious disease team. The main effort was to put Jason Redman back together in the best state possible. The goal was to build the newest, best version of Jason Redman they could.

My wife and I had been given advice early on that we needed to make sure that everyone in the reconstruction process was involved in the decision making, especially at the beginning when we were laying a foundation for the facial reconstruction teams to build on later.

As a Special Operations leader, it made perfect sense to me. When we were conducting operations, we had everyone who might be involved in the mission, no matter how small or unlikely their role might be, involved in the mission planning. From quick reaction forces to aerial support assets, to medevac assets, to intelligence teams, we wanted them all there as we discussed our plan. If we were going to do something that would negatively impact their plan, or if they were going to do something that would negatively impact our plan, we would address it and fix it right then instead of realizing there was a problem midmission and trying to correct or adjust it on the fly.

One of my hospital teams, the oral maxillofacial team, wanted to act independently. I asked them to work with the other teams to make sure that everyone was in coordination. Our first oral maxillofacial team said, "No, we don't need to do that. We don't need to talk to them. We know what we need to do."

I insisted: "No, you need to talk to the larger team to make sure we're on the same page and that they are setting you up for success, that nothing they are going to do will cause you problems for my best outcome with your part of this mission." They refused. I maintained again, they needed to communicate and collaborate. They were angry with me. It became hostile until finally, I just said, "I'm done." I requested a second opinion from a civilian doctor and left the military medical system. It was a clear example of a supporting effort that was out of alignment with the end state.

Effective leaders articulate the main effort clearly. You can help each team member know that their piece is incredibly important, and you can celebrate the individual successes that contribute to the team, but at the end of the day, individuals cannot focus solely on their own accomplishments as if they occur in a vaccum; they must understand that their specific successes must contribute to the main effort. That's what is going to ultimately make the entire organization successful.

NO BAD TEAMS, ONLY BAD LEADERS

WHEN THINGS GO WRONG, WE TEND TO BELIEVE AN EXTERNAL factor or person led to the failure. It was an employee. It was a market variable. It was faulty research. It was negligence by my

XYZ team. And while sometimes those things play a part, as a leader, you have to take responsibility for all outcomes, just as we discussed in chapter 3 on ownership.

When something goes wrong, your first thought should be to examine yourself. Did I set my team up for success? Did I give them everything they needed to be successful? Did I give them the right guidance? Did I give them the right motivation? Did I give them the right training? Did I give them the right resources?

In Jocko Willink and Leif Babin's best-selling book, *Extreme Ownership*, they go into great detail about the power of this principle in leadership and teamwork. They give a fantastic example through a poorly led boat crew conducting surf passage operations during SEAL training. I know this is a common occurrence in young leaders, both in the military and in the business world, as I saw it in action firsthand when I went back to training years later and watched one of the classes conduct surf passage races.

In a similar situation to that Jocko and Leif describe in *Extreme Ownership*, the boat crew teams and their boats were assembled side by side, thirty yards from the ocean. They waited, their paddles at attention.

Suddenly, the instructor yelled, "Stand by. GO!"

Each boat crew grabbed their boat and ran out into the water. They started rowing like crazy. They had to get out past the surf zone, where the waves were crashing. They had to flip their boat upside down and then flip it upright. Everybody then got back in, and they rowed back to the beach. Whoever reached the beach first was the winner.

The winning boat crew got to take a break. Everybody else had to keep doing it. So over time, I watched as the boat crews continued the evolution. In and out. I noticed a pattern start to develop. One crew, Boat Crew Blue, led by Ensign Blue, was winning every race, and another crew, Boat Crew Gold, led by Ensign Gold, was losing every race. The instructors were noticing the level of discontent and arguments that were going on within Boat Crew Gold.

Not only were they losing, but they were losing their composure. Ensign Gold had lost control of his boat crew. The instructors came over and said, "Ensign Gold, come here. What's your major malfunction, dude? Your boat crew's a train wreck, and you guys are losing everything, including your minds."

Ensign Gold replied, "Well, I got a sorry sack of losers with this boat crew. They're a bunch of unmotivated, just terrible people. The whole class would be better if they would just quit." The instructors asked, "Why can't you show your boat crew how to work together like Boat Crew Blue? Boat Crew Blue is squared away. They're motivated, and they're winning every race. What's your problem? Why can't you guys be more like Boat Crew Blue?"

Ensign Gold said, "If I were leading Boat Crew Blue, we'd be winning." The instructors said, "You know, that's a good point. Ensign Gold, you are now in charge of Boat Crew Blue. Ensign Blue, you're now in charge of Boat Crew Gold. Switch."

They started running the races again. Within three races, Ensign Blue was now taking Boat Crew Gold to win. Ensign Gold was now losing with Boat Crew Blue. The moral of the story is this:

There are no bad teams. There are just bad leaders.

Ensign Gold needed to take responsibility for his bad attitude and lack of leadership. We do the same thing as we lead when we think, *If only I had a different team. If only they would carry their load. If only*... These *if onlys* are excuses.

You have to get your head back under the boat of responsibility. Did you do everything you could have to build that team and set them up for success? How well have you articulated the destination? Are you monitoring motivation and resources? Are you constantly communicating the end state, the main effort? Are you giving them the correct resources to get the job done? These things are all your responsibility as a leader.

In an organizational crisis or team crisis, it's even more important for leaders to give constant, clear direction, because we don't plan ahead enough within an organization to manage a large-scale crisis. They are unexpected. After a leader quickly does the initial assessment, there's the initial action, and after the results of that action are allowed to take effect, the leader reassesses.

In business, I have worked with individuals who did not have their head under the boat. And you definitely know when someone isn't pulling their weight, because if you walk around and talk to people, you will hear it from other employees. They're all working. When somebody else pulls their head from underneath the boat, everyone feels the pressure shift to them. It's your job as the leader to address that and not let it go on too long because the longer the rest of the team carries the boat and one person gets a free ride, the more the animosity grows. It throws everything off on the entire team. If I allow that to go on, I'm like Ensign Gold, who is blaming others for failure when it's on me to provide the needed guidance and decisions. I can't put off those hard conversations and decisions just because I don't want to deal with the pressure or uncomfortable discussions, or worse, because I think it will just work itself out. I've got to get under the boat with my team and hold others accountable to do their part.

CHAPTER 10

(RE)FORGE TRUST

To be trusted is a greater compliment than being loved.

—George MacDonald

IN LATE SEPTEMBER 2018, MY FRIEND AND FELLOW SEAL TEAMMATE Congressman Scott Taylor was running as the incumbent for Virginia's Second District seat in the US House of Representatives. He had won the same seat in 2016 by a wide margin, and all the early polls were positive for the election.

Then, six weeks before election day, he got a call in his office in Washington, DC. An assistant said a reporter was on the line and had questions about fraudulent signatures on his campaign petitions.

"Fraudulent signatures?" Taylor asked. He was dumbfounded. Collecting signatures, while an essential part of a campaign, is an easy task. You stand in front of a grocery store, go door-to-door, engage the community, and as a popular incumbent, he couldn't fathom it. Someone had told the press that her old neighbor's signature was on the list, but that person had been gone for three years. Taylor's team checked it, and their data showed that the person voted the year before. Something wasn't right. He sent someone on his team to the house to see if the person still lived there.

They didn't. For some reason, the database was wrong. These things happen sometimes, because when you collect those signatures, you don't vouch for the actual signature; you vouch that you collected it.

But he talked to his team anyway, just to make sure.

"What's going on?" he asked the leader of the team. "What is this?"

"We don't know—nothing's wrong. It must have been a mistake."

He had no reason not to believe them. His team had been working with him for some time, and they were six weeks from the finish line. In his early interviews with the press, Taylor defended his team, reiterating that signature mistakes sometimes happen, but his team had collected the necessary signatures.

The press countered with more questions, including an accusation that a dead person's signature was on Taylor's petition to run for office.

The accusations seemed far-fetched, and he was sure this was just media hype as part of the election cycle. But no matter what the media said or did, Taylor needed the truth.

Taylor confronted his team again. "Somebody needs to start talking—there's something going on here," he asked. No one had an explanation.

As Taylor scrambled to verify the facts, someone in the press showed him the clear discrepancies that proved someone on his team had been lying. It was a blow. Someone on his own team betrayed him. He took decisive action, firing whom he believed was the responsible employee.

The press coverage was brutal—his name was splashed across headlines and nightly news alongside the allegations of fraudulent signatures. And then he had to face his team—the ones left who'd been busting their tails for months and who suddenly had the wind sucked out of their sails. What would happen to all their hard work? And for Taylor, who could he trust to finish his campaign with dignity and the dedication he knew he needed in the moment?

He realized that the scope of the problem had to extend beyond the person he'd fired, so he had to start by getting to the bottom of what had happened.

"The others on that part of the signature team were clearly swept up in it," he said. "For legal reasons, I didn't question them directly, but one of my team leads talked to all of them. The fired leader had exerted influence, and they had felt pressured to go along." Several owned their failure and apologized, ready to make amends.

Taylor didn't have time to wring his hands or wonder what to do about this team. At that moment, they were on the X, and Taylor knew he had to react quickly to get off it. He recognized that his team had worked hard, even if they'd exercised poor judgment, and everyone needed to see him lead in that critical moment.

But he had an excruciating decision to make. Politically, his team had given his opponent ammunition. Ammunition that would draw millions of dollars in attacks, name-calling, and pure demoralization and might potentially cost him a seat he'd been winning in the polls just days earlier. How could he continue to lead when he'd been betrayed from within and lost credibility with the public? Would he drop from the race?

RESPECT YOURSELF

As a leader caught in an ambush, your credibility may be tarnished or gone—sometimes through no fault of your own. Regardless of the circumstances, you have to respect yourself first to lead well. It would have been easy for Scott Taylor to forfeit his self-respect and walk away. But if you don't respect yourself, how can you expect anyone else to?

I sat down with General Stan McChrystal to talk about how to manage self-respect in an organization after an ambush. He said respecting yourself means exercising self-discipline, even when it's not convenient or when it costs something.

"Hold respect for yourself and maintain that standard. Everyone gets broken sooner or later, but when it happens, go back to your values. Don't start at the new lower point, thinking of yourself as worse. Instead, go back to what's important to you and begin to build again from there."

Leaders must hold themselves to a higher standard. If I'm going through an airport and someone is rude to me, my reflexive response is to be rude back. Most of the time I'm able to bite back that initial response and keep my cool, but sometimes, especially if I'm tired, I can snap back. If I can't lead myself from my values while walking through an airport or standing in a line at the coffee shop, I need to reevaluate where I'm leading from.

That same discipline needs to carry into my business space. It's not just about me. "There are a bunch of people dependent upon you being who they hope you are. It's not just those financially dependent, but especially those who are dependent on you to set the example," McChrystal said. Our attitudes, including how well we respect ourselves, are contagious. We'll still blow it sometimes, but we need to have the humility and self-respect to admit it, apologize where needed, and get back to being disciplined.

It's extremely disappointing—conflicting, even—to work for a leader you really admire, to follow their lead, to aspire to their level, to contribute to their success, and then witness them do something dishonest, rude, or wrong. You realize they aren't who they've presented themselves to be. You're in conflict because you want to continue to follow, but now they've made it hard. They've damaged their credibility with you. You'll always wonder when it will be you on the receiving end of such behavior. The leader didn't respect himself enough to be honest, and now you're struggling to respect him too.

If you realize that you have made those mistakes and you need to reforge trust with your team, it's going to take more than an apology—especially if this has gone on for a while. The only way to rebuild trust, according to McChrystal, is consistent future behavior: "You must govern yourself. If someone apologizes to me because they treated me poorly, great, but until they change the behavior, it means nothing. They've got to make a change."

If you've failed to lead consistently, then take the first steps to respect yourself and keep your values and integrity intact as you lead through action.

If you're facing a betrayal like Scott Taylor did, the principle still applies. Respect yourself enough to make the hard decisions, and lead from your values. People will see the respect you hold for yourself and how it aligns with your decisions.

HUMILITY

IT TOOK HUMILITY AND COURAGE FOR TAYLOR TO CONFRONT THE problems in his campaign team. Too many people confuse humility with weakness. As we talked about in chapter 3, the ego can cause us to do dumb things to protect ourselves personally. It can get in the way as we try to lead, too, especially if there has been a breach of trust.

After I returned to Ranger School with a new mind-set and willingness to learn, humility enabled me to forge trust with my Ranger teammates. I stopped trying to convince everyone of my prowess and instead recognized that every single guy around me had expertise that I didn't have.

My Ranger School partner and I were even able to joke about my mistakes during hard evolutions, which required humility.

"Why am I here?" I would ask.

"Because you screwed up," he'd reply.

"Oh, that's right. I'd forgotten." I don't think I realized at the time how verbalizing that truth kept my ego in check while lightening the mood on so many days.

I started to watch and learn from the people around me, and I started asking questions.

Humility opened me up to ask, "Hey, can you show me how to do that?" When I asked others to share their expertise, there was a surprising by-product that I should have figured out years earlier: rapport. My willingness to acknowledge another person's skills and my eagerness to learn from them built trust and relationships.

It was unrealistic for me to expect a leader to be an expert in every single thing they do. Good leaders have an appreciation for the skills they have, as well as those they don't. That's the reason you have a team. You need people who bring diverse skill sets to the team. It makes everyone stronger.

It was freeing to realize I didn't have to know everything. I just needed to trust the guys that I was working with, let them do their job, and not be afraid to ask questions. In return, that built the trust I needed to be a strong team member first, and eventually it would be the key for harnessing the trust I needed to lead.

HARD WORK

WHEN I WAS FIRST COMMISSIONED AS AN OFFICER, I HAD THE misguided idea that, as a leader, I needed to hold control tightly in my hand. I thought I needed to be there representing in every situation. That misunderstanding had led to my failure in Afghanistan.

After Ranger School, as I sought to rebuild my reputation in the SEAL teams, I stopped trying to control everything and focused on trying to learn whatever evolution we were doing at the time to the best of my ability. I knew that to rebuild trust, I needed to expertly lead myself through those evolutions and let my actions and hard work lead by example.

Vince Peterson's words continued to pound in my head: "People will follow you if you give them a reason to." I needed to put in the hard work to convince my teammates that I was worth following again.

Wherever we were supposed to be, I arrived early. Right time, right uniform. Whatever job I was assigned, I did it to the utmost of my ability. One of my main responsibilities was to manage all the administrative requirements of the platoons. Anything related to travel, logistics, lodging, awards, and paperwork. I made sure I was completely squared away with all of that all the time.

Another way I demonstrated hard work was through volunteering. If you look around your team, there are always things that need to be done. I wanted to once again convey, "Hey, man, I'm here. I'll do whatever's needed for the benefit of everyone involved." Those voluntary tasks had the dual benefit of both building the trust of those around me and demonstrating that I had the ability to do the job.

All that hard work began to pay off. Guys on the team began to see that I was reliable. I made sound calls. I demonstrated over and over again both willingness and competency. I was willing to step into harder, more complex roles, and that led to more leadership opportunities.

Around the same time, I had a boss who saw the work I was putting in. He did a good job of teeing me up for success and building my relationship with the team by giving me more and more complex leadership challenges. As we'd go through blocks of training, there'd be evolutions where the training staff had assigned him as the boss. During one full-blown platoon troop evolution where he should have been managing everybody, he stepped back and said, "I'm going to sit this one out. Red, you got this. You're in charge now."

He stepped back and watched with the instructors. That was not only great for my confidence, but it also communicated to everyone, "Hey, this guy is solid. He's making good decisions, and I believe in him." My initiative drew his attention and trust, and then I followed through, making the most of each opportunity.

If you've ever failed in leadership and tried to rebuild your reputation, the natural tendency is to not want to get back out there, because you don't want to fail again, but it should be the opposite. You should be going to your leadership and saying, "Hey. I screwed up, and here's what I've done to fix it. Here's what I would do differently next time. I really want to get out there. I've learned new things, and I want to learn more." Those conversations can only happen after you demonstrate humility and hard work.

BACK TO THE MISSION

SCOTT TAYLOR DETERMINED THAT HE WOULD TAKE CARE OF HIS people and finish the race to the best of his ability, focusing on the issues he'd campaigned on all along. He refused to select himself for failure. He could have quit right then, but it wasn't in his blood. The next day he went into his office in Virginia Beach, and he called his team together.

Everyone was down. He saw the defeat on their faces. He knew that the only way out was to show them through action that they were not defeated. That sort of courage is contagious. If he'd had a defeatist mentality when he walked in, everybody else would have had one too.

"Yes, we just had a devastating blow, but we have to keep going. We are going to drive forward, be relentless, and stay true to what we campaigned on."

He remained positive. He watched everybody to see how they handled it, and over a couple of days, 90 percent of them were fine; they were moving forward doing what they needed to do. A few couldn't move past it, and his campaign had to let them go. Their no-hope attitudes were bringing down the group.

"I completely understood their anger, their grief. We'd all seen our hard work slip away, but at the end of the day, we had to get back to the mission, and anyone not one hundred percent on board had to go."

It was an extremely challenging time, but Taylor wanted his actions to set the example to lead forward. He knew his team was depending on him to set the tone and rebuild the trust that had been lost—not with Taylor but with the team members who'd sabotaged their success. This is real leadership.

He lost the election by a narrow margin, but he refuses to look back and let himself get stuck in the past.

"You can't let failure overcome you and stop you from moving forward or taking other opportunities that are along your path, especially when it's a path you're passionate about. If nothing else, I'll learn from it and keep pressing forward," Taylor said.

Taylor suffered a friendly fire ambush, taking a hit from

someone who was supposed to be on his own team. He didn't waste time attacking or blaming that person for the weeks leading up to and after the election. He walked right back to his team, stated the present conditions, set a course forward, and remained positive. His example showed that he would not abandon them, that he was there and was committed to rebuilding the trust that had been stolen from them. Taylor's resolve and attitude embody the Overcome Mind-Set and the way to rebuild trust after an ambush. He was humble, worked hard, and didn't give up. I know it will not be the last we see of my teammate Scott Taylor.

FAIL FORWARD AND DON'T GIVE UP

How I FAIL MATTERS. PEOPLE ARE WATCHING HOW I HANDLE myself and others after a mistake. When Admiral Bill McRaven took command of Joint Special Operations Command, he felt the weight of making decisions that affected the lives of the men and women below him. It's impossible to do everything right, to make perfect decisions every time, even with that much experience. When you don't get it right, you get incoming rounds of criticism. And those incoming rounds, when you're a three-star admiral, can be from other admirals and generals, presidents, or prime ministers.

On one of the first missions McRaven oversaw, they ordered a cross-border mission from Afghanistan into Pakistan. He had to convince everyone up the chain of command that it was a good decision, all the way up to the president of the United States. Many had concerns. The Pakistanis were ostensibly our allies, but there was a target across the border that McRaven and his team needed to acquire.

They developed the operation, and McRaven briefed it. While there were some who were reluctant, they supported his decision.

The operation didn't go well. Fortunately, the team got back across the border alive, but they got into a pretty significant firefight. The guys they hoped to capture were killed. Within minutes, everyone above McRaven began to question not only the mission, but whether or not he was the right man for the job. McRaven's phone started ringing with calls questioning his leadership. Despite the incoming negativity, he said the call he remembered most came from General Marty Dempsey, who was the CENTCOM commander at the time. McRaven had initially called to give him a situation report, and Dempsey had listened patiently and simply said, "Okay, Bill. Got it. Good job. I know you tried to do the best thing here."

McRaven hung up the phone, and five minutes later it rang again. It was Dempsey.

"Hey, Bill. You sounded pretty down when we talked."

"Well, sir, this didn't go very well," McRaven said.

"Yes, but that didn't make it a bad decision. You're the right guy for this job. You just gotta hang in there."

That was the supporting fire McRaven needed in a tense time, and he drew on it many times in his career, both when he made mistakes and when he had to address mistakes with those under his command.

As a leader, you have to be very careful not to make it personal when you address mistakes within your team. Someone can do everything right, and the mission might still go bad. You address it no matter what and hold people accountable, but the way you do it can build trust when you recognize that people are doing the best they can.

If you let mistakes get under your skin or cause you to have an emotional reaction, you're undermining your credibility. "You can't have a bad day," McRaven said. "If a leader is having a bad day, his shoulders slumped, his face tired when he visits the troops or the command center, that negativity is contagious. It spreads like wildfire."

Furthermore, if you're wasting time on negativity, you're missing ways to learn and grow. Learning is hard. Failing forward requires you to be willing to take risks and learn from them when they don't work. It begins with trusting yourself. After an ambush, your self-confidence is damaged. You don't necessarily trust yourself to be able to even do the job. You question your own abilities.

But failure is a part of life, and you have to begin to believe in yourself again. You have to get some wins under your belt, and that may or may not be back in the same arena that you were operating in. Sometimes it's easier to go elsewhere to find some of those wins. Maybe that's why they sent me to Ranger School, because it required me to get out of my comfort zone. If I could win at Ranger School, I was doing it with strangers and not within my own arena.

You owe it to yourself to try to reforge trust. After a failure or a burnt relationship, we naturally want to avoid those people and places. That little voice in our head tells us we won't be able to make amends or that it won't matter. Sometimes we don't want to reengage, because it will require a humble apology. It's easier to retreat into silence, but a lack of communication will never forge the trust you need to lead again.

Sometimes self-respect, hard work, and humility will still not be enough to fully recover. But if you learn from it and stay true to your mission, you can get up and keep going like Scott Taylor did. He finished his campaign well, maintained his integrity, and will launch into his next venture a stronger leader for the experience.

CHAPTER 11

CLEAR COMMUNICATION LINES

Be silent for the most part, or, if you speak, say only what is necessary and in a few words.

—Epictetus

AS I INTERVIEWED ADMIRALS, GENERALS, COMMANDERS, AND OTHER high-level leaders for this book, over and over they stressed the importance of listening in decision making. It's not that every person always gets a vote in the decision process, but good ideas come from everywhere, and you can't tap into them unless you are listening.

Failing to listen to your team is a surefire way to implode. Just ask my buddy Jocko Willink.

It's hard to imagine Jocko Willink as a young SEAL. I personally feel sorry for Jocko's mother because I imagine Jocko was at least one hundred pounds at birth and came out of the womb in a fighting stance, wearing a jujitsu gi. But alas, the reality is that even Jocko Willink had to learn some lessons as he grew up. He was actually the youngest guy in his first two SEAL platoons, which he described as a great experience for someone hungry to learn and paying attention. He said he learned as much from the poor leaders as the great ones.

In one particular platoon he served with, the platoon commander was so bad that the platoon worked together to get him fired.

"It was the E5 mafia, young enlisted guys that rebelled against the officer in the platoon, which is crazy. You're not authorized to do that." The platoon commander micromanaged, barked orders, demanded respect and got none. Jocko was one of the few in the unit who got along with him, but Jocko recognized poor leadership. "As a young SEAL, I asked myself, 'Why don't I want to follow this guy?'"

As a leader, you are the chief communicator no matter what conditions or barriers exist to complicate your message. Good communication is grounded in clearly articulated goals. Do you know where your team is headed? How will you get there? What is the objective when you arrive? And sometimes most importantly, why does this goal matter? Take time to make sure you understand your goals for your team and why they matter. If you aren't sure, run them by a few trusted friends or mentors first to check clarity.

Too many leaders believe that "because I said so" is motivation enough for their team. What that actually communicates to your team is either, "I don't know why, just do it," or, "I don't care about your intelligence or viewpoint, just do it." Both hurt the reception of your message and ultimately undermine your leadership. There are always situations when you don't have time to explain the why in the moment. That's why you have to be proactive with your self-discipline and listening, so when you make the occasional "just do it" call, you have already built the credibility needed for your team to trust your decisions.

You may be relaying information from multiple sources to your organization. In those cases, it's important to sort through what information is needed by your team. There are countless pressures in combat. You have political pressure pushed down from senior leadership. You have operational pressures driven by your teams. There are tactical pressures, those immediate threats on the ground coming in. There are the external pressures of the enemy soldiers and the civilian population. All of these different groups communicate different information and needs all at the same time. A leader sorts through those messages and holds them up to the mission to see what is priority. As a leader, you have to listen first—to your team, to outside information, to those you report to. Then, you sift through those messages to make sure you have received what you need before you communicate up and down the chain of command to move forward.

SIMPLE PLAN, CLEAR PURPOSE

No matter what you're trying to get your team to understand or do, the most important component is a shared purpose. Just as you had to define your life mission in part 2, you have to be clear about your company's or team's purpose too. Those you lead need to know why the work they do matters in the larger scheme of things. When you listen both up and down the chain of command, either you'll hear a pattern that reveals shared goals, or you'll hear a bunch of people at odds going different directions. If you are leading, don't give an order until you have a clear purpose, and then every action or directive needs to correlate with and contribute to that purpose.

When I spoke with Admiral Bill McRaven about the planning and execution of numerous missions, including raids like the one that killed Osama Bin Laden in May 2011, he said, "Too often, people want to make a complex plan. It's far better to have a simple plan and share a clearly communicated purpose. For the Bin Laden raid, we built a simple plan. Carefully concealed, repeatedly rehearsed, and exercised with surprise, speed, and God knows we had purpose. Everybody on that mission probably would have given their life to get Bin Laden. That's shared purpose."

The mission, Operation Neptune Spear, only took forty minutes from the time they landed on the compound in Abbottabad to the time they returned to base. The entire operation, from the approval by President Obama to the time Bin Laden's identity was confirmed and he was buried at sea, took less than twelve hours. As a leader, McRaven didn't have to communicate the years of data and intel that led to the raid. The SEALs and other supporting elements didn't need a long history lesson or data dump. Their leaders had sifted through the information, identified what was necessary, and communicated a simple plan and clear purpose. Every man on the team could have told you the singular, focused purpose of that raid: kill the world's most wanted terrorist. And they did.

Talk to your team. Do they know the purpose of your company or organization? How do the tasks they do daily align with that purpose? Evaluate how well you are sifting information to get the most timely, relevant details to your team. Extraneous information will muddy your purpose and increase the chances that your mission will fail. Keep the plan simple. Get clear on purpose and communicate roles and tasks in relationship to that shared mission.

VERIFY MESSAGE RECEIVED

ONE NIGHT IN LATE JUNE 2007, MY SEAL ASSAULT TROOP HAD BEEN assigned a target. We patrolled through the humid Iraqi summer night, passing through desert terrain, past plowed fields, irrigation canals, and villages before we arrived on the outskirts of a small village where our target compound was located. Our troop split into three assault teams; each would take down one building in the compound.

As we closed in, we walked by a house that was about sixty yards from the target. Two individuals slept outside. They looked harmless enough, but we took no chances. I didn't know if they were innocent bystanders who might get hurt in a scuffle, or if they were armed, dangerous insurgents who would complicate our mission.

We needed to make sure those two sleepers were secure before we went in after our target in case anything went south.

I turned to the Iraqi leader we were working with.

"Put two guys on those sleepers. Wrap them up and secure them while we take down the primary target."

He nodded.

"Are you good?" I asked.

The response came: "Yep, I'm good."

"Roger that."

We moved to the final set point, a small shed about fifty yards from our target, a one-story square concrete structure with a porch that ran around the entire house. We did a last-minute check of our gear, our breachers prepped their door charges, and everyone gave the good-to-go signal. The execute call was given, and we descended on the compound. The enemy always gets a vote, though, and all hell suddenly broke loose.

There were enemy fighters on the roof who began dropping grenades on us, and a machine gunner also on the roof came alive. We were taking gunfire from multiple positions behind us. Sleeping in the courtyard next to the house were eleven women and children ranging from a newborn to an eighty-year-old woman. Our enemy was raining grenades on us and the Iraqi women and children. We quickly rounded them up between the explosions and herded them into the house and out of the immediate fragmentation area. My primary interpreter was caught in one of the grenade blasts, peppering him with searing hot metal fragments. He had multiple blast injuries and one large piece of molten-hot metal that had torn into his neck. He shrieked in pain. Additionally, two of my teammates were hit with frag and sustained minor wounds.

On a scale of calm being zero and insane chaos being ten, we'd just hit fifteen. Our team took very effective fire from various positions. There were multiple wounded, and the Iraqi women and children were screaming and crying inside the house. I calmed my racing mind and focused on my most immediate problem. I had to take out the enemy shooters that had us pinned down. In order to do that, I needed to get a full head count so we could call in the fire mission. My medic was corralling our wounded guys and treating the interpreter, who was in danger of bleeding out.

I listened to the chaos on the radio between explosions and bursts of gunfire while I continued running around, trying to get a full head count. But I kept coming up one guy short. The blasts and bullets ricocheting off the building made it hard to communicate, and we were running out of time to act. But we had to make sure we had all our people accounted for.

I quickly thought back through the communication between our team members and had a nagging hunch. Maybe the Iraqi team member hadn't understood my command and still had an extra guy back there, and not in the compound currently under fire. The Iraqis I'd left holding the sleepers did not have radios. I had to make a decision. Do I grab one of our men and tell him to go back to the house and confirm my suspicions? I looked around, and all my guys were 100 percent engaged in a fierce firefight, controlling the Iraqi family, or taking care of our wounded. I also knew that whoever I sent would be exposed to heavy machine-gun fire and grenades from the enemy barricaded on the roof. That did not sit well with me. How could I communicate with our other elements and get the head count I needed? Where had my communications gone wrong?

My primary job was to get the head count, so I decided I was the best man for the job. I took a deep breath, let my team leader know what I intended to do, yelled at one of my machine gunners to destroy the rooftop with cover fire, and ran as fast as my battle gear–laden body could go.

Thankfully, I did not get blown up or cut down, and I made it through the sixty-yard sprint to the other house. Sure enough, my Iraqi leader had put himself and two other men on that house instead of the two I had initially instructed. This mis-communication cost almost five additional minutes of confusion and could have cost lives. I should have clarified with my Iraqi leader that he understood where to go once the two sleepers were secure. Instead, he stayed with them, adding up to three people holding our sleepers instead of two. More importantly, I should have gotten a final head count at the set point before we started the assault. I would have realized then that we were missing one man. I had put us in a tough spot trying to clarify our head count in the middle of an ambush instead of making it crystal clear before executing.

BARRIERS

ONE OF THE BIGGEST BARRIERS TO CLEAR COMMUNICATION IS assumptions. People make assumptions about the speaker, the message, the intent, and their own reception of the message, and each of those assumptions holds potential for a breakdown.

As a leader, check your own assumptions first and start from the belief that everyone is trying to do their best with what they have, based on the information and resources they have. Too many leaders assume someone is being lazy or defiant when they don't follow directions the way you want. Instead, ask questions. Find out why they acted in the manner they did.

As leaders, we wrongly assume our teams know everything about us. No one can read your mind. No one will view a situation or decision exactly the way you do. So stop expecting them to. You can spend a lot of time breaking down barriers, but the best way to get clear lines of communication is to build rapport with your people through open communication. Strong relationships are forged through solid communication. In the military, rank, structure, and the rigidity of the organization allow you to get away with being very blunt and direct sometimes.

In the civilian world, I came to learn that rigidity does not work. Everything in the civilian world is built on relationships. I got out of the military and was very task focused. It took me a while to understand that I needed to take the time to build relationships, get to know people, learn about their families, and understand who they are. When your people know you care about them, that you take the time to ask after their spouse or kids, they are far more likely to listen when you speak about business matters.

LISTEN AND LEAD

FOR JOCKO, AS HE WORKED TO UNDERSTAND THE POOR LEADERSHIP and communication of that platoon commander, he finally saw some patterns emerge. It boiled down to the same things. The platoon commander was arrogant. He wouldn't let them participate or give them any ownership of what was going on. He didn't listen.

"When he got fired, he came to me and asked me what was going on. I said, 'Sir, you don't listen to anyone.' It was hard to watch, but it was a good lesson for me.

"The officer who replaced him was awesome. He was great at everything that we did, every physical activity. He was a great shooter; he was a great leader. Everyone respected him. He set the example.

"That officer inspired me to become an officer because he had been a prior enlisted guy. And when you're in a SEAL platoon, the SEAL platoon is your whole world. That's the only thing you care about. When he took over that platoon, he made the world good for the sixteen of us in that platoon. And I just remember thinking to myself, Someday I'd like to try and make the world good for sixteen men."

If you run a company, a team, or an organization, your primary focus should echo Jocko's goal: to make the world good for your team. A key part of setting an example that people want to follow is listening. You can rule with an iron fist, like Jocko's fired commander, but you'll be fighting your team the entire way, wondering who is loyal. That isn't leadership. Real leadership cares for the health of the whole organization and each person in it. There will still be failures, but you listen and let others give input.

Your business or family communications might not be life-or-death situations, but they may very well be the difference that makes a marriage last or keeps a business solvent. As I saw with my miscommunication with the Iraqi team member, you can fully understand the mission, have a solid plan, and communicate that plan with all the people on your team, but if it is misunderstood or ignored by even one person, it will cost you in the long run.

It's essential that you take the time to know your team, to practice communication, and to have protocols in place to help you detect when there is a breakdown in communication. At the end of the day, as a leader, it is your job to go back and check that the clear plan is being executed. With time, trust, structure, and procedures, you will know these things are being done, but a leader spot-checks to confirm accountability. When you communicate a new plan or a change, ensure your people are practicing active listening, in which they repeat back your message to make sure it is clear. Sometimes you will realize that part of the message has been missed, as in the case with the mission I discussed earlier with our Iraqi team members and the sleepers.

Communication is an ongoing exercise in relationship building and good boundaries. If you've struggled to assert yourself or you find others won't ask helpful, clarifying questions because you have an iron grip on the helm, it's time to release your control and get back to clear communication protocols and listening. When your team has a shared vision, a clearly communicated, simple plan can deliver the results you've been pursuing for years.

CHAPTER 12

EXECUTE AND STAY THE COURSE

Success is the sum of small efforts, repeated day in and day out.

—Robert Collier

I STARTED MY FIRST BUSINESS RIGHT AFTER I BEGAN APPEARING in public with my injuries. People stared. Children pointed. It irritated me. They didn't care that I was that military member in dress blues and sharp uniforms they loved to cheer. They only saw my injuries, the broken outside. Those voices from the hospital, the ones who showed blatant pity, resurfaced in my memory. I refused to let that be how I was viewed. I started printing T-shirts to educate the public about why I might look a little different. The designs had an American flag and the words WOUNDED WEAR on the back. On the front, I printed statements such as:

STOP STARING. I GOT SHOT BY A MACHINE GUN. IT WOULD HAVE KILLED YOU.

SCARRED SO THAT OTHERS MAY LIVE FREE.

SHOT FOR YOUR FREEDOM. JUST SAY THANK YOU.

The first time I wore one of the T-shirts through the airport on my way to Chicago, I noticed a difference in how I was viewed and treated. Some of the awkwardness was replaced with appreciation. I felt like I had taken a conscious step toward controlling a situation that was definitely not in my control. We opened shop in 2009 and called it Wounded Wear. It provided the creative release I needed, as well as the visibility and awareness we needed as wounded warriors. It was a positive outlet while I was recovering.

My board and I made the decision to morph Wounded Wear into the Combat Wounded Coalition, a newer expanded version of the nonprofit, and we hosted events such as Toast to the Heroes, bringing in hundreds of wounded warriors and Gold Star family members from across the country, and Jumping for a Purpose, where we took wounded warriors, their families, and Gold Star family members and let them jump out of perfectly good airplanes for charity. We connected wounded warriors to needed resources by vetting and identifying good, proven veteran nonprofit organizations. We raised money for the SEAL Foundation and other organizations in our community.

With the help of my alma mater, Old Dominion University, the nonprofit also helped us develop our Overcome Academy, through which we teach wounded warriors the leadership skills and Overcome Mind-Set that had helped me survive and thrive.

But by 2018, I got a call from the board chairman of Combat

Wounded Coalition, asking to meet. I knew we needed to talk. A number of things had kept coming up at the company's meetings: our dwindling resources, my speaking schedule conflicts, the medical liability concerns for our Overcome Academy. But I was determined to keep investing in our wounded warriors. The need was so great, and I felt I had a responsibility to lead through the nonprofit. I refused to quit. Quitting wasn't an option.

But during our conversation, the chairman said, "Jay, this is good work, but we can't continue to do this in this way. We don't have the resources, and I'm worried about you burning yourself out."

My instinct was to fight it. We'd been in situations like this before where I'd charged back in, committed to making it work, saying, "We're gonna fight. We're gonna keep it afloat." But I was beginning to see from the business side that we couldn't do it in a healthy way. We'd gone through that cycle several times. I realized that I was at a decision point once again. In order to save the organization, I would have to shift all my time and energy to it. I either had to stop speaking and totally focus on the organization, or I had to shift focus full-time to speaking because I was doing a half-assed job trying to do both.

But I don't quit.

That was the thought that kept rattling around in my mind. Any fallback felt like failure. I kept thinking through all the evolutions we'd been through to get to that point. I didn't want to let down the families of the wounded warriors we'd supported. I didn't want to pull back from the results we were seeing in so many veterans who were taking back their lives. It had come so far from that first iteration I'd begun years before.

How could I give all that up? The thought was excruciating.

But if I focused solely on the nonprofit, I couldn't take care of my family. For years I had made the conscious effort not to take any kind of real salary from the nonprofit. My take-home pay for an organization with nine employees was $1,600 a month. Even with my retirement pay, it was not nearly enough to take care of a family of five, so it left me constantly scrambling to supplement my income.

As I sat with my chairman, replaying all the ups and downs we'd come through, I couldn't imagine shutting it down. But I didn't know how we would keep it going either.

"Shouldn't we stay the course?"

"But at what price?" came the reply. I had some thinking to do because we needed to act, and fast.

TIME TO ACT

EXECUTION EQUALS ACTION. THE TIME TO PLAN IS GONE. IT'S TIME to trust yourself to lead again: not plan, not strategize, not talk—act, and as you lead others, it's time to trust them to do the jobs you have set before them. Mistakes will happen, but as long as you continue to press into your purpose with clear goals and communication, your Overcome Mind-Set will carry you off the X permanently. Recognize that action doesn't have to be large-scale, sweeping action to make a difference. In fact, more often than not, it's the small, one-degree turns over time that change the course of a ship or company.

I knew this from my experiences at Ranger School. The end of Ranger School was only the beginning of my redemption. It had been an opportunity to prove to myself that I could be a leader worth following. It was challenging, humbling, and ultimately life changing. I had a clear course returning to the SEAL teams. I wanted to regain the respect I had lost. I knew it would be an uphill battle to earn back the respect and trust of my teammates, but the real test would come if I was able to lead effectively again.

It took over a year and a half. I had succeeded at Ranger School and grown exponentially, but as soon as I stepped foot back into the SEAL teams, I knew I was starting over again. I couldn't walk in and say, "Well, guys, I got myself straightened out in Ranger School. We're good, right?" No. I had to prove that I had changed through daily action and sustained superior performance over time. I had eyes on me—waiting to see signs of the old, impulsive Red. He was still there, of course, but he was tempered, refined. I was 100 percent committed to letting others see the change in me.

Each day, each week, I watched for small wins to help me keep going. Those small things—being on time, working hard, having a teachable attitude—began to have a cumulative effect. I found myself in more conversations. I had a teammate seek my advice or expertise. I got a slap on the back. These don't seem like much, but after being ostracized, I knew what connection and respect looked like. I finally reached that redemption point when the silence broke and guys were joking with me again. There were even a few affirming words after training missions: "You did a great job."

There were so many times during those intervening years when I thought, *I don't know how I am going to pull this off*. But I had to stay the course, just continuing to focus on one evolution at a time. I had to lead myself first. People are going to follow you when you're leading yourself well.

I've returned to those values again and again whenever I've had a setback or failure. Each time there was a moment of doubt, I'd remind myself of the journey back to being a leader in the SEAL teams. I had done it there, and I could do it again in business and life.

It's the same thing within an organization or company. There are things you can't control. What you can control is your reaction to them. So often I wanted to respond negatively, but for what? I would think through the consequences of that. How's that going to impact me? How's that going to impact my team?

If it's just getting hard, but you are making progress, that's the time to lean in and keep going. Be the boat crew leader who continues to guide the ship while trusting and motivating your team to do what they've trained for.

DECENTRALIZE POWER AND LET OTHERS LEAD

You've spent a ton of time developing your team, forging trust, and articulating the new mission. But it won't do any good unless you trust them to act without your micromanagement or constant interference. When I sat down to talk with Jocko about this, he explained that he guides his own business by maintaining that balance of authority, using the same strategy we used in defeating counterinsurgency in Iraq: a decentralized command. In a traditional military hierarchy, the general is at the top, and then the various levels of ranks stack below him, each subordinate to the one above. Decisions typically come from the top down, with each level carrying out the command to a tee. There is little space for discussion, and not following orders can result in disciplinary action or release.

Al Qaeda doesn't work that way—they don't play by the rules of engagement, and they are extremely agile in the way they are able to attack. The American military had to make a significant change in the way it operated to be able to fight the extremists. As a result, we worked in smaller interconnected teams, sharing more information more quickly, so that targets were not gone by the time we secured approval for engagement. We decentralized authority and focused on making sure the mission was absolutely clear in any area to enable ground commanders to make calls more quickly in line with established goals.

Jocko describes how he uses the same principle in his business now:

"I've got multiple components working together, but I have key trusted personnel inside all those different organizations that are taking the lead and running. They need very little guidance from me other than broad strategic advice about direction. Occasionally I have to step into the details for clarification, but usually I don't have to. I have a factory up in Maine, and I've got a guy that runs the factory up in Maine. I've got a supplement brand. I've got a guy that's running the supplement brand. We've got Echelon Front. I have my team at Echelon Front that make things happen there.

"With everything that I do, I've established a great co-leader in all these different organizations, people that I trust that I can use decentralized command and make all these things happen.

It's [the] exact same thing as when I was a platoon commander, when I was a task unit commander, when I was in charge of the training command. I wasn't going out and running every block of training. I couldn't do that all by myself obviously. All these people step up and make things happen."

Jocko has set the standard for execution. He selects and trains the people he needs. He communicates the mission clearly, and he executes. Full speed ahead.

TAKING THE DIFFICULT COURSE

WHEN I TOOK A STEP BACK TO ASSESS, I REALIZED THE GOALS I HAD set for myself with the organization, alongside the other things we were doing, were unrealistic. It wasn't good for me or my family. Something had to give. I had a decentralized command in my business, but there were multiple essential components that required me.

What was my purpose? Who was Jay Redman, and what did he want to contribute? I am living a second chance so many of my fallen teammates did not get. I want to take the lessons I have learned and help make people better. I want to share my experiences and knowledge to give the next person the strength and tools to get off the X and reengage their life. The nonprofit was not the best way for me to execute that course anymore. My course had changed. But still, I didn't want to quit.

It was a hard decision because, technically, I had to quit something. It was unsustainable. I relied heavily on my board to help me be objective. I talked through each scenario with them. No choice was going to feel like a win, but we had to make the best one based on the intel we had, the outside perspectives we sought, and the goals of the organization.

It's like flying an airplane when all the alarm bells are going off, telling you it's going to crash. Your options are to land it safely right now, or run the risk of hoping somehow you can repair it in the air, and if you can't, you catastrophically crash. Sometimes we delay execution, which can cause us to either miss opportunities or crash entirely, making the situation worse. I knew it was time, so I committed to helping my staff find new jobs and continue paying the ones who helped with the shutdown of the organization.

I selected the best of the bad decisions. We decided to step back from the organization. I hated every minute of closing it down, and it still stings when I think about it. Not because we failed, but because we succeeded so often through the really difficult work despite the failures. The nonprofit had forged me for my next evolution. I had to execute this new direction and stay the course.

As I released the nonprofit, I realized that all the work, all the material we'd developed was still valuable. I could still help people with the training I had developed. I just couldn't keep doing it the way I was doing it before.

I have talked to people since then who have confirmed our decision, saying, "Hey, there are plenty of times in business where quitting is the right decision. If it's not sustainable—you're losing money, and you're losing resources—then yes, it is time to stop doing it."

My chairman, Doug Porter, a very accomplished business-man in both the for-profit and nonprofit worlds, agreed. He told me, "There's a life cycle to everything. For every organization there is a beginning and an end. This ran its life cycle." It was hard to admit because I have this relentless Overcome Mind-Set that said, "We can do this," but I finally stepped back when I accepted that I couldn't live there. The tempo was just too high, and the cost was outside my purpose and goals.

Sometimes execution looks different than you expect, but that's why you spend time building a team, forging trust, finding a mission, and communicating. Now it's time to stay the course.

OVERCOME

THE LAST COMPONENT OF EXECUTING IS BOTH SIMPLE AND DIFFICULT: you stay the course. You overcome. You don't give up. The road you've chosen to execute will likely be hard, especially after a crisis. Other obstacles are bound to pop up. Often the path off the X is excruciatingly hard and fraught with danger, but I guarantee the journey is worth it.

It takes discipline to stay the course. This is why so many people have problems executing or creating lasting change. They identify what needs to be done. They make a plan. But for most people, it dies there. They're not willing to take action. For the few who are willing to take action, too many don't have the discipline when it gets hard.

This is where you need your Overcome Mind-Set. This is where the Pentagon of Peak Performance has trained you to stay the course. Mental leadership and emotional leadership truly build our ability to withstand discomfort and change. You're never going to have a 100 percent effective solution, but if you have planned well, using all your resources and connections wisely, then it's time to act, knowing you will likely have to make adjustments as you go.

When you expect your execution to need adjustments, when you know it's going to be hard, you mentally prepare yourself for any obstacles that could come your way. That's how you persevere. That's how you stay off the X and move forward. That's how you lead others. You have all you need to conquer this journey. Assess. Commit. Act. Overcome. It's the only way to rise above survival and truly thrive after an ambush, and you will become a leader worth following to the end.

PART 3 DEBRIEF

- To lead, begin by getting your head back under the boat, carrying your weight, and being clear about your role.
- To reforge trust with your team, respect yourself with humility and hard work. When you fail, acknowledge it and keep moving forward.
- Learn to clearly communicate by listening, and build relationships that will minimize barriers to communication.
- Once you articulate the mission, it's time to execute and persevere. Take that first step and trust your team to do what you've trained them to do.

IMMEDIATE ACTION DRILL: REACT

Part 3 challenges you to get back to leading after an ambush. Take a few minutes to REACT.

- **Recognize your reality:** Who are you leading, and what is your mission? What would success look like?
- **Evaluate your position:** What challenges do you face as a leader? What challenges within your team will you need to address to complete your mission?
- **Assess possible exit routes:** Look back through the chapter titles for this section. Which one do you most need to address? Do you need to redefine or clarify roles in your leadership team? Do you need to practice active listening? Make a quick list of the three most pressing problems your team is facing and possible solutions to try.
- **Choose a direction and communicate it:** Pick one of the solutions you listed. If you don't know where to begin, start by listening to your team. Ask them what the most pressing issues are and how addressing them would improve your business or organization.
- **Take action:** Try one of the solutions THIS WEEK. Don't put off that hard conversation. Apologize if you've been in the wrong. Clarify the mission and take the first steps. If you run into an obstacle, engage your Overcome Mind-Set and push through—encourage someone else on your team to keep going when it gets tough.

PART 4

LEAD ALWAYS

CHAPTER 13

CULTIVATE GOOD ORDER AND DISCIPLINE

Through leadership we will inspire others to success.

—Jason Redman

IN THE EARLY 2000S, ADMIRAL BILL MCRAVEN MADE A VISIT TO AN outpost in Shkin, on the border of Pakistan. It was our farthest, most remote outpost. There was no running water. Every night, troops took shelter from incoming rockets from sympathetic Taliban fighters, led by the tribal leader Haqqani. It was a brutal environment.

On this particular visit, McRaven accompanied a two-star Army general who was in charge of the war in Afghanistan. When they arrived, they walked into a room where a SEAL team member had been assigned to brief them on the status of the outpost.

"The general and I were in desert fatigues," McRaven told me, "the appropriate uniform for the region and time of year. The SEAL was sitting at a table in the room when we entered. He wore jeans and a shirt and a giant bushy beard. I waited for him to stand and salute the general. Instead, he remained in his seat. 'I understand you guys want a brief?' he said."

Guys?

You're addressing a two-star general and a one-star admiral and you call them *guys?*

McRaven didn't flinch.

"Yes, we do," McRaven replied, as he and the general took a seat.

The SEAL introduced himself by his first name, and then gave a half-assed brief, just enough to provide the necessary information.

"Thank you," the general said, rising to leave. McRaven stood too. The SEAL, though, didn't. He kept sitting in his chair. Ignoring the broken protocol, the general turned to leave. McRaven hung back. Should he blast this SEAL on the spot, or just let it go?

The conditions at Shkin were harsh. Few people from outside units, let alone top-level officers, *ever* visited. The soldiers inside the outpost were under constant assault from all sides. Plus, while the SEAL was out of uniform, it wasn't as uncommon as you might think, since many Special Forces units, not just in Shkin but all over the battlefield, had grown beards and adopted more casual dress to adapt to the region and locals.

At the same time, the situation felt unprofessional.

The question was, How important is the right uniform and proper address when you're getting shot at every day? Can you really require that level of discipline and professionalism in a place with no running water, where survival is a daily worry?

COMPLACENCY

ONE OF THE MOST SURPRISING BY-PRODUCTS OF SUCCESS IS complacency. It's easy to slip into success and think the hard days are behind you. A missed day in the gym becomes a week. You have one cheat meal, and the next thing you know, you're eating unhealthy meals regularly. You let down your guard at work and don't complete the quality-control protocols as rigorously as usual and then suddenly notice your employees are skipping protocol too. A little success leads to a little complacency, and over time, your readiness suffers. You worked so hard to get out of the last ambush, but now you're putting yourself at risk again.

The only way to lead long-term, to lead always, is to maintain the habit of self-discipline. "Discipline equals freedom," as Jocko Willink says. Otherwise, you become enslaved to your old habits, laziness, and mindlessness. If something is easy for too long, you should immediately see it as a red flag. "Easy" will not produce the results you want.

Furthermore, you don't always get to pick and choose when you're going to lead. There's no leadership highlight reel where you get to choose the moments you'd like people around you to see. They see it all: the good, the bad, and the ugly. They know if you are saying one thing and doing another. Every action you take is an opportunity to lead, if you are willing to embrace it.

LEAD FROM WHERE YOU ARE

ADMIRAL ERIC OLSON IS A PERFECT EXAMPLE OF SOMEONE WHO stepped up to lead in extraordinary circumstances during the Battle of Mogadishu in Somalia in October 1993. The battle is dramatized in the 2001 film *Black Hawk Down*. I sat down to talk to him about his leadership at Mogadishu during the most deadly operation the US had seen since Vietnam. Olson had been sent to Somalia to gain experience on the ground, and his first duty there was as a watch officer. He ran the Joint Operations Center (JOC) eight or twelve hours a day in Mogadishu. They ran a series of raids to capture the lieutenants of Mohammed Farah Aidid, who had been responsible for the Pakistani ambush that led to the UN mandate for his capture. Olson had been on that duty for a few weeks when they began an operational raid on a house where two of Aidid's key lieutenants were meeting.

"It was supposed to be a routine grab-and-go mission, but two of the helicopters involved were shot down by RPGs in short order about thirty minutes apart in different sections of the city," he said. The two-star general in command above Olson suddenly had a complex set of escalating conditions: a diverse cadre of vehicles and troops to coordinate due to the UN involvement, and people on the ground engaged in combat at the crash sites. "It seemed as though everybody in the city had a gun in their closet and was out in the street, which made the rescue missions even more dangerous," Olson said.

One of the helicopters was shot down in a fairly remote site with no way to reach it over land. Michael Durant, the sole surviving crewman, was injured and trapped in the cockpit, facing down a horde of militia headed his way. Two Delta Force snipers, Master Sergeant Gary Gordon and Sergeant First Class Randy Shughart, watched the scene unfold below them from a nearby helo and had to request permission to go in to provide ground cover three times before they received the go-ahead, and they hit the ground to defend the Black Hawk and Michael Durant long enough to save his life, even as they both died in the effort.

The other helicopter was shot down in a more urban area, closer to where the ground operation had been inserted. The armed civilians and militia made ground movement slow and dangerous. "I went from being a JOC chief to being the liaison for the mechanized element, because I spoke Arabic, which was helpful for coordinating the tanks and mechanized elements, which included Pakistanis and Malaysians," Olson said. He worked alongside the Army, as well as other relief forces, to transport the trapped, wounded, and dead from the crash sites. Olson, along with five other SEALs, would later be awarded the Silver Star for conspicuous gallantry.

Olson cited the heroics displayed by numerous units during the fifteen-hour conflict. "In the chaos, people reverted to their training, and training got them through the harrowing and fast-paced reaction. The scene itself was so chaotic that it was hard to develop, communicate, and execute a coherent plan. It was people at every level making decisions that affected them and the situation directly around them."

That training and instinct saved numerous lives at Mogadishu. Whatever untenable conditions you are facing, step up and lead from where you are. Offer your expertise and professionalism like Olson did. When you draw from your self-discipline and your relationship with your team, you can overcome any obstacle that comes your way.

DEMAND GOOD ORDER AND DISCIPLINE

As MCRAVEN STOOD TO LEAVE WITH THE ARMY GENERAL ON THE border of Pakistan, he made a quick decision to demand good order and discipline.

"Would you give us a minute, sir?" he asked the general, who stepped outside.

McRaven called the senior chief to attention and outlined his expectations clearly.

"I have higher expectations for one of my SEAL brothers, Senior Chief. We stand when someone of a higher rank enters the room. We look sharp and professional. We are prepared and impressive. Even in these harsh conditions. Understood?"

"Yes, sir."

After he left, McRaven contacted the commander of the unit from Dam Neck, Virginia, and reamed him. "If I ever see one of your SEALs act like this again, he's out of here and you'll be with him."

McRaven continued to depend on good order and discipline as his career went on. A few years later when McRaven became the commander of Joint Special Operations Command in 2008, the first thing he did when he arrived in Afghanistan was order the beards cut.

One of his senior officers replied, "Sir, we need to talk to the enlisted guys first. We need to study this."

One week later, the senior officer came back after talking to all the senior enlisted guys.

"Sir, I'll be damned. They want to cut their beards," he said.

McRaven wasn't surprised. "They join the teams to be somebody special. If they're in beards and jeans and they aren't being the soldiers and sailors they joined up to be, then they need to go. Good order and discipline begins with holding them accountable for their grooming and uniform requirements—in boot camp and now." McRaven got his point across, and everyone shaved.

When leaders let things slide, when you allow small side steps, you are undermining the very training your team needs to make it through tough situations. In a firefight, like the one in Mogadishu, people reverted to their training, and it was essential for every person to do their job. McRaven knew it was his responsibility to hold his people accountable for what was expected.

Leaders set the compass, and the compass bearing has got to be true. Good order and discipline, particularly in the middle of combat, matter. Being professional matters. Doing things that are moral, legal, and ethical matters. Leadership matters. Character matters. Because if you lose your bearings, you're never going to reach your objective. When everybody understands what's expected of them, and you as the leader hold them accountable, then you'll be able to follow that compass to true north. If not, the unit won't perform, and you won't be able to get out of that ambush zone when it comes.

Return to that foundation every morning and drive toward your purpose. It starts with you. Don't allow complacency to seep in and steal your professionalism and effectiveness.

CHAPTER 14

PURSUE MARGINS OF PEAK PERFORMANCE

Leadership is a journey that never ends. There is no finish line in the race to be a good leader.

—Jason Redman

PRIOR TO 9/11, THE DIFFERENT SERVICE BRANCHES' SPECIAL Operations units competed for missions, since there were relatively few assigned. For that matter, there's always been a level of competition between conventional forces and Special Operations. Each group tried to position itself to get that airspace. Sometimes the conventional forces would get it. In the early '90s, the SEAL teams were much smaller and less recognized than our Army Green Beret brethren. Sometimes it felt like we were the forgotten stepchildren.

At that time, as we competed with the Green Berets for more assets and missions, it grew ugly, and we didn't play well together. One time when I worked in Special Operations Command South, a plane crashed in Colombia. The Army wanted to recover it, but it had crashed in a remote location of Colombia that was controlled by the FARC (Fuerzas Armadas Revolucionarias de Colombia—Colombian guerrillas). There was some sensitive equipment on that plane, so they wanted us to sneak in, secure the crash site, and extract the equipment.

It was mountainous, rugged terrain, and we had just completed two weeks of vertical assault training, a really fancy military description for proficiency at climbing mountains. All our gear was good to go, everybody in the platoon was fresh, and all of us had the climb training, including how to set up rope systems to navigate and recover the sensitive equipment in the rough terrain.

We submitted our concept of operations to the general in charge, and the Army Green Beret unit stationed down there did the same. They didn't have the training, and we found out they didn't even have the gear to do it. We checked our gear and prepared to be sent out.

We didn't get the mission. Not only that, but the Army general made us give the Green Beret team our gear for the mission.

How could we have been passed over? We were the best team for the job with the best training and the best equipment. How could we convince the higher-ups to see how our elite performance was right for the job?

We were shocked and angry to have been passed over. But the bigger question was, How could we become the best force on the field if we weren't recognized as such? We *believed* we were the best. We had the best training and the toughest, strongest men in the military. And yet, despite all that, we were *still* passed over. Beyond politics, how could we prove we were the best, the elite, the top 0.1 percent?

And for you, how do *you* compete at that level? Not just *compete* but *win*? How do you become the best in the world?

MARGINS OF PERFORMANCE

JAMAICAN SPRINTER USAIN BOLT THRILLED THE WORLD WHEN HE broke his own world record for the hundred-meter dash at the Beijing Olympics in 2008, dropping his time from 9.72 to 9.683 seconds. A year later to the day, he would take to the starting blocks again in Berlin and drop his time to 9.572. Impressive to say the least, and a terrific example of how small margins make a big difference. Bolt is considered the fastest man on earth as of this writing, with his speed hitting over forty-four kilometers per hour (over twenty-seven miles per hour) between the sixty- and eighty-meter mark of the race. The world record set in 1964 by Bob Hayes was 10.06. Usain Bolt's world-record time forty-five years later would be less than half a second faster. Half a second.

That tiny margin of performance separates the excellent from the elite.

What would have happened if Usain Bolt had decided that 9.72 was good enough? We wouldn't have seen the two additional records he broke recorded during our lifetime. There's danger in settling for good enough—in letting down your guard and deciding that you don't need to push anymore. Sometimes a plateau is a signal that you are quitting mentally, which is the first sign that your body is going to follow. Commit to constant incremental change instead, and draw on both competition and mentors to take you to the next level.

INCREMENTAL CHANGE

KAIZEN MEANS TO USE SMALL STEPS TO MAKE IMPROVEMENTS, OR TO use small moments to inspire innovation. You may believe you have to make a huge leap to see progress, when the reverse is actually true. Real change, lasting change, happens in the small, consistent moments that build over time.

Kaizen (*kai* = change, *zen* = good) is a Japanese term, probably best known for its use at Toyota after World War II when the car manufacturer began its quality circles, or groups that met regularly to analyze and solve problems. Toyota used these groups to focus on small incremental change over time, which ultimately led to the company's superior quality.

While the principles of *kaizen* were designed to improve manufacturing, they highlight the process all of us can use to improve ourselves, our relationships, and our businesses as we try to beat plateaus and complacency. You can use a similar process to evaluate where you can make small habit changes that will over time yield larger cumulative gains. Some of the principles of *kaizen* include the following:

- Commit to continuous improvement.
- Never keep an idea just because that's how it's always been done.
- No blame. No excuses. They only stall improvement.
- Abandon the belief that something new is always going to work.
- When something goes wrong, correct it as soon as you see it.

- Welcome ideas from everyone to solve problems.
- Identify root causes. Ask why over and over until you've framed the problem correctly.
- Improvement is a moving target. You'll never arrive, so keep pushing.

So many of these principles are key in SEAL teams. If you read about *kaizen* at length, you'll notice that there is a focus on eliminating waste as well as adding value. When we're looking for an edge, we want quick fixes, like a new supplement or a magic pill. But subtracting low-value activities from your life and business can accelerate your performance as much as adding to your regimen.

Kaizen requires continuous improvement and constant monitoring. Be the person on your team or in your organization who is focused on solutions and productive questioning.

When I showed up at the doctor's office in 2015 and he hit me with the potential-heart-attack bat, I realized I had to make some major changes, and quickly. I began to look at what was impacting me: stress, negative people and influences, lack of sleep, no fitness program, and excessive amounts of alcohol. I immediately looked at what I could cut: alcohol, negative influences causing stress, things that hindered my ability to go to sleep. Then I focused on what I could add to my life that would begin some momentum: start and stick to a fitness routine and a sound diet and surround myself with positive people. As I spent time in each area of the Pentagon of Peak Performance, I began excelling, but I also noticed that I had to get more concentrated with my focus on eliminating the negative margins and increasing the positive to see higher returns. The margins of performance were at work in my life.

EVALUATING MARGINS

To evaluate your business margins of performance, examine those areas that positively or negatively impact your goals. Maybe it's a meeting you have every week that you require every single person in the organization to attend, but in reality you're only talking about marketing and sales most of the time. Your IT and accounting people don't need to be there. It's a waste of their time. That's an example of a negative margin of performance, because those team members could be working on other things that are actually moving the needle for your business.

Once you've identified what those margins of performance are, find ways to tweak out the fine levels. Which projects, processes, and products are creating a drag on your resources? How can you free up time? What are you doing at those razor-thin margins that are moving the needle one millimeter at a time but that add up to exceptional gains?

It's that half a second for Usain Bolt. Maybe it was genetics. Some of it was how he trained. But how did he squeak that out? He kept training. He stayed focused, and he sure didn't settle for good enough. He even competed with himself to beat his Beijing time.

MENTORS AND PEERS

The people around you will make a huge impact on your margins. "You will be the same person in five years as you are today except for the people you meet and the books you read," said Charlie "Tremendous" Jones.

In the Pentagon of Peak Performance, social leadership is your ability to connect with people and maintain and leverage these relationships for your own good and the good of others. Look around. Who are the people you're surrounding yourself with? Who is mentoring you? How intentionally are you building networks of people?

If you are showing up to conferences and events, that's a great first step, but you need to be intentional about initiating relationships with people who are focused and moving in the same direction you want to go.

At a recent event, my own mentor challenged me in this area. "Are you spending time with other people that run high-level businesses?" my mentor Bedros Keuilian asked.

It struck me then that, no, there are times when I wasn't being intentional enough about the people I surround myself with. I wasn't intentionally asking questions about the best practices in other industry leaders' businesses.

Are you spending time with the people in your industry who are the elite performers, the ones innovating every day, making changes and reinventing their field? It doesn't matter if you're in sales, management, or making coffee. If you want to become one of the elite, you need to start spending time with them first. You need to surround yourself with people who are operating at the level you aspire to operate at.

The right people raise you up, and the wrong people will pull you down or, at least, keep you stuck in the status quo. Who do you think you should be spending time with? Now is the time to find them and start building relationships with them.

UNHEALTHY COMPETITION

When the green berets got that airplane-recovery mission, we were bitter.

Later, that same team reached out to us and said, "Hey, would you be willing to teach us ship-boarding tactics?"

What we should have said was, "Of course. If we teach you what we know, and you teach us what you know, we'll both get better."

What we *actually* said was, "Screw you."

It seems childish now in the aftermath of 9/11, when we fought alongside each other with mutual respect. We missed an opportunity to build those relationships in Colombia. We could've looked at the shared training as an opportunity for the future. And if we had done that early, we could've been better prepared for the onslaught of joint missions that were necessary after 9/11.

When the climbing mission came up, we could have said, "Why don't we put together a joint team? You have a great plan and a few subject-matter experts in climbing. We have the training and the gear. Let's get this done together."

But instead of working together, we were afraid of them stealing our airspace. *We* were the subject-matter experts when it came to ship boarding. We were so far ahead in ship boarding that the chances of them being picked for a mission requiring it would be slim. We should have looked further down the road, recognizing that it would have built rapport and could've set us all up for success later.

Competition can be a motivator that helps you pursue the

margins that make you better, but beware of letting ego keep you from learning from your competition. Our refusal to work with the Army Special Forces made both groups weaker when we both had the same big-picture mission.

To be the best, you need to learn from the best and keep working at it every day, never settling. Often, that means your biggest competition can be your best teacher. Don't make them the enemy. Instead, dump your ego and focus on getting better.

Usain Bolt never settled for second place. He kept looking for ways to maximize his assets and shave off those milliseconds that consistently crowned him champion. You can do the same in your business and life if you adjust what you think is possible and commit to leveraging those margins of performance that will make the most difference.

CHAPTER 15

LAUNCH FROM ADVERSITY

The only thing stopping you from accomplishing greatness...is YOU. It doesn't matter the color of your skin, where you were born, what size you are, or your sex. Greatness is within you. It's up to you to release it.

—Jason Redman

AFTER A LIFE AMBUSH, WE EXPECT THINGS TO RETURN TO NORMAL. It's understandable but usually impossible. It's also a missed opportunity. Our great power lies in launching from adversity in a full embrace of what you've learned from it.

In the early days of my recovery, I was hell-bent on getting back to being operational. I hated being separated from my team and the mission, and I focused entirely on returning to them as soon as I could. Once it became apparent that I'd never get full mobility back in my arm, I had to confront the grim reality that my operational days were done. I shifted my goal to finishing my twenty years in the Navy, working to support my teammates and their families to the best of my ability.

It would take me several more years to fully understand the value I could offer others as I launched from adversity. One such iteration resulted in an intensive fourteen-day course I called the Overcome Academy. I knew my never-quit attitude and strong Pentagon of Peak Performance saved my life in that ambush in Iraq, and I was determined to help others get off the X and begin to live again.

Our first class came through Virginia Beach in February 2018, and we began leading wounded warriors back to their purpose to launch their own recovery and new missions. Just like my Sign on the Door stated, as wounded warriors, we don't want your pity. We don't want your condolences. You have no idea what we have seen in defense of our nation or what we have endured on your behalf. We only want your respect, understanding, and support. Most importantly, we want the opportunity to achieve our own successes, our own versions of the American Dream, despite our injuries. The Overcome Academy teaches our wounded warriors how to lead themselves and go after that opportunity, and that first class included wounded warriors on both ends of the spectrum: those who had found a way forward and were honing their missions, and those who were still stuck on the X trying to find new purpose. Two of our graduates, Mike Schlitz and Ozzie Martinez, sat down with me to share their inspiring stories of how they launched new lives from their adversity. I hope their stories will motivate you to begin telling a new story in your life too.

BURNED BUT NOT BEATEN

US ARMY SERGEANT FIRST CLASS MICHAEL SCHLITZ SAT IN A DONATED private jet in November 2007, trying to keep from shifting in his seat. Every move caused friction between his still-healing skin and the head-to-toe bandages that encased 85 percent of his body. He'd suffered burns when an IED blasted him from his Humvee in Iraq months before. He shoved the pain away and focused on seeing his platoon again. Just the thought of them continuing the mission without him had been excruciating. *But I survived*, he thought. There were three in his team who had not, and their losses weighed heavy on him. Soon he would see the rest of his platoon as they returned from Iraq, the men who had saved his life just nine months before.

Mike deployed with the Army's 10th Mountain Division out of New York to Baghdad in August 2006. Their platoon spent six months running patrols, and then in late January, they switched with another team to do road sweeps for IEDs. They had a cadre of up-armored vehicles for the job, including a Buffalo with a claw for extraction and several Huskys to help detect the mines buried along the roads.

There are two ways to find IEDs. One, your equipment detects them and you call an explosive ordnance disposal (EOD) team to come out and defuse them. Or the IED finds you when you roll over it and it explodes. Many IEDs are smaller devices that just damage the vehicles, and Mike's platoon had seen their fair share of vehicle damage over the month they'd been working along the roads in their assigned area. His mechanics were having trouble keeping up with the pace of repairs.

By mid-February 2007, they had so many vehicles down that Mike had no choice but to take his commander's Humvee and put it in the convoy. As platoon sergeant, he made it his vehicle and put it near the back of the convoy. They weren't seeing a lot of vehicles in the back get hit, so he felt confident they could make it work until they got their vehicles back on the road.

They ran missions for about a week with that Humvee in their convoy. On February 27, they were out on a fourteen-hour mission when they rolled slowly down a dead-end road, scanning the road, the shoulder, and the horizon.

"All clear." The word came, and they turned around at the dead end. They headed back up the road at a faster speed and rolled over a deeply buried IED that contained two artillery shells and a propane tank.

When the IED detonated, it sprayed shrapnel, and Mike's Humvee caught on fire. The propane tank blasted through the floor of the vehicle, killing the gunner and medic instantly. Mike's driver was pinned in from the blast and couldn't escape. On impact, Mike's door blew open, and he was thrown from the vehicle ablaze.

Mike jumped up to run and check on his comrades, and he felt the flames lick at his face. He was on fire. He dropped to the ground and rolled, the heat searing across his skin, sizzling in pain. But the propane was an accelerant, and with every rotation, Mike reignited until his muscles locked up, and he stopped facedown in the dirt, burning alive.

I'm going to die here, he thought, the pain greater than anything he'd ever imagined.

Suddenly, he heard his guys yelling from the other vehicles.

Before he knew it, they were spraying Mike with the fire extinguisher. The physical relief was immediate. Mike shifted from the most intense burning pain he'd ever experienced to feeling like he'd had an ice blanket laid on him.

Thank God, he thought. *My guys are here. Maybe I'm not going to die. Maybe there's a chance.*

Even smoldering on the ground, he began trying to give orders, setting up security and calling for the reports to begin. The guys were already on it—training had kicked in, and everyone sprang into meticulous, ordered action. Within ten minutes the medevac landed. The flight medic got his name and then the morphine hit. Mike was out and would remain under for the next four months, his only recollection a single flash from a gurney while he was being transported from Landstuhl, Germany, to Brooke Army Medical Center in Texas.

Nine months had passed since that day in Iraq. Nine times he'd flatlined on surgeons' tables in Baghdad, Germany, and Texas. He lost both hands to the burns. Countless times he'd fought infection, pain, depression, and anger. He wasn't sure who he would be now that he wasn't an active-duty Ranger anymore.

Mike's mom and brother had been beside him nonstop through the first six months of his recovery.

"What will I do now?" Mike asked from his hospital bed. "My military career is over." It had been a dark time, wondering how he would ever fully recover.

"Maybe you'll write a book about your experiences," his mom encouraged him. "Or maybe you'll begin speaking publicly, telling your story."

He laughed bitterly. The last thing he wanted to do, even

before he was horrifically burned, was speak publicly. Now, with so much of his body burned, he definitely didn't want to be on a stage. He just wanted to get back to his platoon.

Every day that he'd been conscious, he'd thought about his guys, and now, because of the generosity of Veterans Airlift Command, he was able to travel from Texas to Fort Drum, New York, where his unit was returning. He was accompanied by his mother, a doctor, and a nurse who would provide near round-the-clock bandage management, physical therapy, and monitoring during the trip.

On the morning the platoon's flight landed, Mike sat in his wheelchair, biting back the pain and fatigue, excited to see his men. As they filed off the plane, he wished he could fully return their salutes at attention. They'd planned the customary welcome-home ceremony and get-togethers, and Mike attended as well as he could.

But fatigue set in early.

His wound care and physical therapy took him away from the festivities.

He'd been able to show them how he could take a few steps, but then he'd slumped back into his wheelchair. The emotional toll began to wear on him. He was incredibly proud and relieved to be with his men, but he was frustrated at his own exhaustion. Frustrated at his inability to stand and lead from the front. His energy was completely sapped.

I'm letting them down, Mike thought. *I am letting this be a weakness. I have let go of my discipline while I have been surviving. Rangers lead the way, and I can lead if I adapt to this new reality.*

Mike returned to Texas with a new mission: get back to his self-discipline and the military mind-set that had made him a successful Ranger. Within a couple of months, he'd ditched the wheelchair. He quickly progressed from walking to jogging, getting back in physical shape. He continued to lean on his huge support network of family and friends who had been unwavering through his ordeal while he battled the anger and depression that accompanied his recovery, and he rediscovered his purpose.

Once he was medically retired, Mike got a call inviting him to speak at an event. He ignored the fear and went. He told his story, and it ignited the fuse that would become the next iteration of his career. Word got out about his inspiring story, and he continued to accept invitations. People were hungry to hear about what was happening in Iraq from someone who'd been there. He kept talking.

Soon, Mike was being invited to paid corporate events, and he immediately noticed problems in leadership in those companies. The basic leadership tenets he'd learned during his military career weren't being followed. Leaders weren't taking care of their people. They were either disengaged or micromanaging. It opened Mike's eyes. As an infantryman, he knew the retirement plan for most in infantry entailed contracting or security detail, but he realized that he had much more to offer.

His speaking topics broadened, and he began teaching the basic leadership principles he'd learned as a platoon sergeant and sharing the lessons he'd gleaned at Ranger School. He built his business from the ground up, remaining positive and inspiring others to overcome difficulties and embrace real purpose.

In 2017, Mike accepted a full-time position at the Gary Sinise Foundation as their military and veteran resource manager, where he continues to serve and inspire everyone he meets. His role connects veterans and their families to resources, helping them find their purpose, but he cautions his clients, "You can't teach anything you haven't been through yourself. Ranger School taught me that my mind quits before my body has to. It was a lesson that carried me through ninety-six surgeries and the recovery and therapy necessary to reengage my life. Don't become overly dependent on others. You are in charge of your life—you are the one who can lead yourself into your future."

Mike is an astonishing example of launching from adversity. He travels the country evaluating and helping nonprofits through his job with the Gary Sinise Foundation. He motivates and inspires other people. He's got a great attitude. Others in our Overcome Academy looked to him as a perfect example of how to get back to your life purpose and serve others at an elite level.

FROM FRONT LINES TO TIGHT LINES

OSVALDO "OZZIE" MARTINEZ JR. DROPPED TO HIS KNEES IN THE shower one morning in 2014, begging God to take his life or change it. Separated from his wife and son, designated as 100 percent disabled due to PTSD, he felt utterly alone, and he was only sure of one thing: something had to change. He had been living too long in a dark, isolated existence, unable to move forward with any purpose.

Marine Corporal Martinez completed two deployments to Iraq from 2004 to 2006, serving in a dangerous and deadly Fallujah, where his unit saw life-altering casualties and humanity at its worst. He separated from the military in 2006, but he was reactivated in 2008 to train Afghan soldiers, and that's when the anxiety and panic attacks began. Before he knew it, he'd received a letter that he was no longer fit for active duty and given a 70 percent disability rating for PTSD and sent home. The job he'd been pursuing as a police officer had received the same report about Martinez's mental health and dropped him. The losses from Iraq, the pointlessness of civilian life, and the lack of direction mounted. He was beginning to understand the desperation twenty-two veterans a day experience: enough dark to snuff out his own life.

"I couldn't get past the survivor's guilt. I was depressed and completely stuck."

A couple of weeks later, a buddy from his unit in Iraq called him out of nowhere and invited him to come up to his cabin in California for a reunion with others who'd served alongside him. Martinez agreed to go, but in his mind, he went to say goodbye.

Martinez spent a week remembering old friends, laughing, and realizing he wasn't alone. So many of his comrades were experiencing the exact same disconnect from civilian life, isolated and unable to outrun the demons of war. He went home at the end of the week with a phone full of contacts who knew where he'd been, and a sliver of hope that things might get better.

Back in Miami, Martinez wanted to recreate the sense of community he'd felt at that California reunion. A lifelong fisherman, he organized a fishing trip with other veterans. He recognized the therapeutic effects of the sport as well as the opportunity to share what he loved about it—the thrill of adrenaline while pulling a huge sailfish or mahimahi from the water.

"On a boat, I have a captive audience. People have time to talk and listen, which is important because PTSD is so misunderstood by the public and even those who have it. I shared the positive adrenaline rush I got from sailfishing, and I knew that more veterans needed the opportunity to experience a positive outlet like that."

On June 1, 2015, the first day of National PTSD Awareness Month, Martinez opened his nonprofit: Operation WetVet, a 501(c)(3) nonprofit out of Miami. His goal is to help combat-disabled veterans with PTSD and traumatic brain injuries make positive memories in a safe environment, and to remind them of two things: to manage your PTSD, you have to be honest with yourself, and you have to cultivate a community. You don't have to be alone. You're NOT alone. Martinez encourages every veteran who sails with him to contact the people from their old units, because no one else will understand like those comrades will.

"I went to all kinds of therapy when I first got out. Most of it wasn't helpful at first. In group sessions, we might have had the same symptoms, but we hadn't gone through the same things. It felt like no one really understood. It was important to me to talk to the guys who'd lived through that experience in Iraq because they knew what we'd survived."

The nonprofit began to fulfill its mission, but Martinez was still living alone, separated from his wife. He'd found purpose in Operation WetVet, but he was afraid to scale. Organizations would call to contribute and media attempted to promote his work, but he deflected. "A big part of PTSD is the instinct not to trust. Any new information can be challenging to process because your brain tells you to reach for safety—to protect." Martinez found himself living but not yet thriving, because he was unwilling to open himself to risk.

In 2017, Martinez's friend Shawn Lopez recommended that he attend the Overcome Academy. Lopez had just completed the inaugural class, and he encouraged Martinez to go and learn how to scale his business if nothing else. Martinez went.

"It wasn't life changing—that was up to me—but it was absolutely mind changing. That's what I needed. To get off the X, I had to get honest and get going with my goals. The class gave me a framework and the tools I needed to launch."

At the end of Overcome Academy, Martinez had set three goals and finally publicly told his story in front of his academy comrades. His wife walked in moments before it was his turn to speak, which amped up an already emotional event. Still, he stood up, and for eighteen minutes, he told his story, the real story of how he struggled with survivor's guilt and the weight of all he'd seen to the point that he'd sat in a shower contemplating the end. "We're taught to be strong—to show no weakness. I'd told surface stories from Iraq about other people, but never my story." He felt like an elephant had been lifted off his chest and he was able to capture his first full breaths of air.

As he left Overcome Academy, he made some courageous decisions. He asked his wife to go to therapy with him or divorce him. They'd been separated for two years, coparenting his sons, but Martinez wanted to stop living in limbo. She agreed to go to therapy with him, and they reunited soon after. The three goals he had set during the academy included enrolling in college, growing Operation WetVet, and the one that really scared him: considering politics. "People don't have to be so divided, and we have to work to understand each other better," he said.

A year later, he's enrolled at Miami Dade College, he's an active member of the student government association, and he has begun branching out with speaking and scaling Operation WetVet. Scaling and speaking in front of larger audiences brings on new problems and challenges, but Martinez is committed to overcoming them.

"Every day I make the choice to keep moving forward. I'm not letting myself retreat and get caught on the X again. For too long, I was creating barriers in my mind because I was afraid of risk. Now, I know I have to choose to act despite those fears."

He is absolutely on fire, taking back his life and living out his mission. His honesty about the past has opened a whole new future for him, one that isn't lived in isolation anymore.

IGNITE YOUR LAUNCH POINT

A LIFE AMBUSH IS MISERABLE WHEN WE GO THROUGH IT. MAYBE WE don't fully recover from it, but it creates a whole new path. So many people get stuck on what they lost or what they no longer have. They want the past so much that they're not willing to turn around and look forward at what is in front of them. They fail to even consider, "Okay, what are my new opportunities, and could something better come of it?"

Once they finally begin to move forward, so many find out that their crisis point becomes a launchpad. I can't tell you how many wounded warriors I have worked with say, "Despite the pain, despite the miserable journey, this was probably one of the best things that could have happened to me." I know I am one of them.

Crisis, adversity, failure. Life ambushes are some of our greatest teachers. They forge the Overcome Mind-Set. They teach us perspective. They teach us outlook. They teach us gratitude. They teach us the value of life that most people take for granted.

Sometimes a life ambush will end a career or mark a significant shift in your life, as it did for me. As I recovered from my injuries, a near-constant concern was how life would look after I fully retired. Retirement left me with free time and uncertainty about what to do next. A number of opportunities presented themselves, and I was worried that I only had a small window of time in which to grab them. I wanted to charge hard after anything that popped up, to make sure I wasn't missing out. I ran from one event or project to the next, hoping something would bring me purpose and set a direction. I threw different ideas at the wall, hoping one would stick. It was a lot of trial and error for a while, instead of identifying my purpose and destination and then comparing opportunities to see which ones would best get me there. After talking to thousands of retired military guys, I think we often fall into that trap. We're going after everything, frantically searching for our new mission and purpose, and so many of us can't figure out why we can't make things stick.

When I talked with Bill McRaven about this challenge of purpose, he spoke candidly about his surprise that the now-viral commencement speech he gave in May 2014 made such a wide-ranging impact, leading to his book *Make Your Bed*.

"I always thought my purpose had been to be a good SEAL,"

he said, "but after that speech, I realized I could have a far greater impact. Being a four-star SEAL was simply a springboard to do something good and inspire people." That desire to do good for others is at the heart of service, and coupled with a strong moral compass, it can take you far, even if the road is interrupted by obstacles, failures, and ambushes.

After you get out of the immediate chaos and pain of an ambush and get to a breathing point, it's time to do that assessment of who you are and what you want to have accomplished or who you want to be by the end of your time here. I call this your life's mission objective. It is the legacy you will leave behind. A life ambush is the perfect launch point to define your purpose and life's mission objective.

There will still be grief, denial, and anger, but those who launch realize there's an opportunity. That negative experience can not only make you better, it can make others better. You can make something positive out of what happened.

The sooner you get off the X, the sooner you get to that point where you are actively looking for ways to use the experience to help others, and the sooner your new purpose and mission will come into focus.

Don't self-select yourself for failure. Choose to have hope, and understand one key fact: hope is an ember, an ember that you can ignite into a raging inferno. It's contagious, and others can't help but be motivated and inspired by it. This is the fire on the launchpad. And the sooner you see the ignition point, the sooner you can find your fire starter and begin your bonfire of hope.

That's where you can truly thrive. Launch from adversity, and see where it takes you.

PART 4 DEBRIEF

- Counter complacency with self-discipline. Always.
- Evaluate the margins that can take you from excellent to elite and actively work to get better daily.
- Harness your adversity to launch into the next iteration of your life. Don't hold back!

IMMEDIATE ACTION DRILL: REACT

Part 4 challenges you to beat complacency by committing to continuous improvement through self-discipline. Take a few minutes to REACT.

- **Recognize your reality:** When do you tend to fall into complacency? Are you still harboring any part of your ambush and letting it hold you back?
- **Evaluate your position:** What part of the Pentagon of Peak Performance tends to be weakest and when? In what area are you coasting, even a little? How comfortable are you talking about your ambush and how you've begun moving off the X? Is there something you've been dreaming of doing but haven't allowed yourself to begin?
- **Assess possible exit routes:** What would it look like to use what you've learned from your ambush to help others? Make a list of possible avenues. Do you need to tell your story? Do you need to call up others who you know are suffering from a similar ambush? If pursuing a dream, what is the smallest first step you could take? Maybe it's enrolling in college, like Ozzie Martinez, or considering that invitation to speak, like Mike Schlitz.
- **Choose a direction and communicate it:** Choose one area to amp up this week, or choose the smallest (or biggest!) step you could take toward your dream.

Write down your plan for addressing it and give it a deadline.

- **Take action:** Take a deep breath, lean into your Overcome Mind-Set, and take the risk needed to push out of complacency, inaction, or fear. Do it today.

THE ONLY EASY DAY WAS YESTERDAY

Tomorrow always will come. It is up to you to be ready for it, to shape it and make it what it will be.

—Jason Redman

IF YOU'VE MADE IT THIS FAR, I JUST WANT TO SAY CONGRATULATIONS. My mission with this book is to help you get off the X, rediscover your mission in life, and launch into your future.

But I have some bad news for you: it never gets easier. You'll be tempted to slip back into a weak mentality at times, thinking things should get better, easier. You might grumble about a bad day because you missed a flight or the barista got your coffee order wrong. You need to redefine what a "bad day" looks like and broaden your perspective as you continue to drive forward.

What privileged Westerners view as a bad day is nothing in comparison to what daily life looks like in some places of the world.

When I was with the SEAL teams running counter-drug missions down in South America, my eyes were opened to the reality of how bad a day can get for so many in our world. I saw people living in cardboard boxes on the side of the street, men and women who were disheveled and dirty, kids running around naked who were just skin and bones. The stench was overwhelming. I remember watching one of the kids pick up some trash from the street and lick the residual crumbs or sticky leftovers from the wrappers.

In Colombia, a man walked into our camp one day with a three- or four-year-old girl who had severe third-degree burns from her waist down to her midthighs. It looked like she'd been set into a pot of boiling liquid. The man carrying her in claimed he was her uncle, but he didn't seem that concerned about her. His attitude seemed to say, "I've got this problem that needs to be fixed: take her."

The girl was in critical condition, and we wrapped her for transport.

"Where's the closest hospital?" we asked our Colombian counterparts.

"Fifteen miles by boat," they told us.

We loaded her and sped down the river. Once we arrived, we rushed to the building that they said was a hospital. Even from the outside, it reminded me of something out of a B-grade horror movie. Despite the poorly lit hallways, we could see it was dirty and completely unsanitary.

We carried her into the operating room in disbelief. The medical tools were rusted. The hospital staff took over, so there was nothing more we could do. We left, and I thought to myself, *Oh my God. How can she survive under these conditions?*

When we went back to check on her several days later, the dressings were soiled and hadn't been changed. The hospital didn't have any to use on her wounds. We returned and brought a bunch of dressings for the young girl. After that, I don't know what happened to her. I knew infection would likely set in without proper care. Had she been in one of the larger cities, she might have had access to better care, but here, deep in the southern Colombian areas controlled by the FARC, she had little chance of pulling through.

There are parts of the world that rarely, if ever, have access to what we would deem necessities.

Running out of gas, a delayed flight, or a missed dinner are inconsequential in comparison. I hear a lot of people joke about "first-world problems." They don't know how sad the truth of that statement really is.

You have to maintain perspective as you face each day after an ambush. Your loss, failure, or grief might be profound and paralyzing, but you can hold out hope that you understand the fragility of life better because of your experiences. You have more to offer the world because of what you've survived. It won't be easy, but I can guarantee you'll be stronger. You just have to keep that Overcome Mind-Set with each evolution of life.

I've talked with young wounded warriors, middle-aged executives, retired generals and admirals, and all of them have one thing in common. Change happens. Some of it will be good. Some will be bad. Some will be incredibly painful. If you maintain the status quo, those external influences—the "enemy"—will create changes without you. And often they will be negative changes. Instead, go back to your values, what you stand for. Go back to the life mission that will get you up in the morning. Keep your head up, look for the worst-case scenarios, and evaluate constantly. Keep getting better, pressing into discomfort, finding those margins of peak performance. Build your Pentagon of Peak Performance and keep it strong. This is the only way to overcome. If you don't overcome every day, the world will overcome *you*. And then it's only a matter of time before a life ambush takes you down.

There's a saying in the SEAL teams: The only easy day was yesterday. It doesn't mean that the easy stuff is behind you. It means there are always more challenges ahead. Yesterday only seems easy because of the way you are pushing yourself today. Most people hope to make their lives more comfortable day by day. They want to do things the way they've always done them. What they don't know is that if things are easy, life is probably about to get hard. If you are comfortable, you are in danger and likely not ready for the next ambush on the horizon.

If you're reading this book and you believe in this message, though, you know comfort is a myth, a temptation. It will only bring you down. The Overcome Mind-Set requires perpetual challenge. Resist settling for what's easy. Ask yourself, How do I push myself a little harder? How do I do things just a little better? How can I make one small improvement in one area of my life today?

The SEAL teams constantly change our tactics, because we know comfort and the status quo are the enemy. At times, we'd step into a situation where what we were doing before didn't work anymore. We had to adapt and change. You can too.

If you do it right, you're always pushing, never peaking.

You're constantly trying to change. And change sucks. Nobody likes change, because change is hard. It takes work and patience, and it's uncomfortable.

But that's what ambush survivors do. That's how they overcome.

Congratulations, you made it! But it's not the end.

It's just the beginning . . .

As the SEAL ethos says, you have to "Earn your trident every day."

For all you reading, you have to "Earn your leadership every day."

See you out there on the Battlefield of Life.

Lead always and overcome all,

JCR

ACKNOWLEDGMENTS

This book would not have been possible without the support of my friends, family, and warrior teammates.

First and foremost, I want to thank my Long-Haired Admiral and best friend, Erica. You have been beside me through every life ambush and you never batted an eye. My story is as much yours as it is mine. You make me better.

To my incredible children: my man cub (now a man, but always my man cub), Crooked Styles; my angel, Angelica; and my princess, Mackenzie; your love brought me home and sustained me through all of my MAJOR life ambushes. Each of you is growing up now and setting your own paths. I will enjoy watching you chart your courses and navigate your journeys. Go forth and lead yourselves, lead others, and lead always. Most importantly, never feel sorry for yourselves. Get off the X and Overcome. This world will give you nothing and you are entitled to nothing. Earn it. Be a victor, never a victim. Always remember, I love all of you and I'm so proud of you as a Dad.

To my father and stepmother, Roger and Betsy Redman, thank you both for being there for me and raising me right. I love you both.

ACKNOWLEDGMENTS

To my mother, Colette Redman, thank you for always supporting me and my dreams. To this day, you are still my biggest fan.
Thanks for being my Mom. I love you.

I wish to express thanks to my brother and sisters, Selby,
David, and Renee. All of us have been through our fair share of
life ambushes. Perhaps this book will help all of us get off the X
and find greater successes! Love to all three of you.

Special thanks to my SEAL, Special Operations, and Warrior
brothers who contributed their incredible stories of leadership,
discipline, overcoming, and getting off the X to make this book
as powerful as it is. A HUGE and heartfelt THANK YOU to Admiral Eric Olson (Ret), Admiral Bill McRaven (Ret), General Stan
McChrystal (Ret), CDR Mark Divine (Ret), LCDR Jocko Willink
(Ret), former Congressman Scott Taylor, Sergeant First Class Mike
Schlitz—US Army (Ret), Corporal Ozzie Martinez USMC (Ret),
and Sergeant Shawn Lopez USMC (Ret).

I wish to thank everyone in the SEAL teams whom I had
the honor to work alongside and who helped grow me into the
man I am today. To Captain Vince Peterson—you are one of the
greatest leaders I ever had the honor to work with. Even today I
reflect back on your leadership and example for guidance.

To the men of One Troop—thanks for giving me a chance when
you knew the baggage I carried coming back from Afghanistan.
KD—thanks for being a great mentor, leader, and friend. You
live the principles I speak on now. Al and Pat—thanks for being
great friends throughout the workup and deployment and still
today. Al—thanks for running forward to drag me out when I
moved too slow. To the rest of the men of One Troop—thanks
for giving me a second chance; you were the greatest task unit

and platoon I ever worked with in my entire career and I was honored to live, train, and fight alongside all of you. I learned more about leadership working with all of you in training and combat than most people will learn in a lifetime.

I want to recognize my staff and all the volunteers as well as the dedicated patriotic Americans who helped support Wounded Wear and the Combat Wounded Coalition. With your help we were able to support thousands of wounded warriors and raised almost $3 million over the life of the organization. Shutting it down was one of the harder decisions I have made, but I know I can go on to motivate and inspire even more through this decision. I learned from all of you and thank you for standing by me while I learned the business world and navigated some of the hard lessons of nonprofit management and leadership. Thanks specifically to Kenny Miller, Danita Jacobs, Michelle Roth, Danielle Becker, Dani Herring, Brooke Juhas, Tisha Sweeney, Rob Allen, Christine Conley, Patrick Brown, Nick Pierce, Donnie James, Kristina and Jimmy Halleran, Dan Jacobs, Renee Knesek, Megan Thomas, Victoria Arboneaux, Eric Wickham, Dr. Glenn Goldberg, Erin Barclay, and Anne Barclay.

Special thanks to my Board of Directors who stood by me in one of my MAJOR life ambushes—Paul Ekoniak, Allen Fabijan, Duke Ingraham, Nancy Lacore, Wil Zemp, Amanda Nesmith (Candor), and our final Chairman, who became my mentor and friend, Doug (AIRPAC) Porter.

Thank you to the Old Dominion University psychology department with all your invaluable research and assistance developing the Overcome Academy: Dr. Michelle Kelley, Dr. Konstantin Cigularov, and Phillip Dillulio. Without your help, Overcome

Academy never would have been. Although the program may have ended, with your help I learned more about the needs of our wounded warriors and how we as Americans can help them better navigate the post-war civilian world.

To the graduates of the Overcome Academy—all of you challenged me, motivated me, and inspired me. So many of you have lived the very intent of the Overcome Academy. You are now out there setting the example in all you do—to lead always and overcome all.

Multiple graduates I talk about in this book; AMAZING individuals who live the Overcome Mind-Set and have REFUSED to sit on the X. Thank you to Tyler Southern, Mary Dague, Mario Spencer, Natalie Lopez, Mike Schlitz, Shawn Lopez, and Ozzie Martinez for allowing me to share your inspirational stories.

To my new Team Overcome—you are all helping me build an empire to help people Get off the X, Lead Always, and Overcome All. Thanks to Jake and Morgyn McCluskey, Eric Wickham, Ryan Golden, and Lindsey Hartz. Here's to changing the world— getting one person off the X at a time.

Thank you to my teammate and friend Ray Care for joining forces with me to spread a positive relentless message to help people Overcome and Conquer every aspect of their lives through our podcast, the Overcome and Conquer show, and thank you to Ryan Davidson for using his AMAZING audio super genius skills to produce our show.

I want to thank my new friend and mentor, Bedros Keuilian. You have the heart, soul, tenacity, drive, passion, leadership, and resiliency of a Navy SEAL. I would be honored to fight alongside you and am honored to be learning from you as I walk this entrepreneurship leadership path and grow my empire to help people become the best versions of themselves.

I want to thank all the companies, organizations, teams, and individuals who allowed me to come in and share my story. I am thankful I got a second chance and I am still here to share my story and provide inspiration and value to people all across this country.

Thanks to my agent, Scott Miller, and the team at Hachette Book Group. Thanks to all of you for believing in my concepts of Overcoming and Getting off the X and helping me navigate the often turbulent waters of book publishing.

Last but not least, to my new friends and talented writers, Joe Bunting and Sue Weems. The two of you were awesome to work with and helped make *Overcome* as powerful as it is. I hope we will impact and change for the better millions of people through this book. I could not have done it without both of you.

Thank you.

ABOUT THE AUTHOR

Jason Redman joined the Navy on September 11, 1992, and spent eleven years as an enlisted SEAL. He was selected for the Seaman to Admiral commissioning program and attended Old Dominion University, graduating summa cum laude in May 2004. He completed his time with the Hampton Roads Naval ROTC as Student Battalion Commanding Officer before he was commissioned as a SEAL officer.

Over the next four years, Lieutenant Redman completed combat deployments in both Afghanistan and Iraq. On September 13, 2007, outside of Fallujah, Iraq, Lieutenant Redman's assault team came under heavy machine gun and small arms fire and he was severely wounded in the ensuing firefight. While recovering at Bethesda Naval Medical Center, Redman authored and hung a bright orange sign on his door, which became known as the Sign on the Door and became a statement and symbol for wounded warriors everywhere.

In 2010, while still on active duty and recovering from his injuries, Redman founded the Wounded Wear™ clothing line and the Combat Wounded Coalition™, a nonprofit organization that inspires combat wounded warriors to Overcome. Redman served as the executive director of the organization for almost ten years. The organization raised almost $3 million and served thousands of wounded warriors.

In November of 2013, after twenty-one years of service, Redman retired from the Navy and launched SOF Spoken LLC, a speaking company that provides inspirational presentations on leadership, teamwork, and overcoming adversity for businesses, first responders, sports teams, and government organizations.

Redman published the *New York Times* bestselling book *The Trident: The Forging and Reforging of a Navy SEAL Leader*. His first book details lessons learned in leadership and overcoming adversity throughout his SEAL career while also discussing his combat deployments in Afghanistan and Iraq as well as his personal journey with his wife, Erica, and their three children.

Today, Jason has expanded his programs with his focus on helping individuals, companies, and teams to "GET OFF THE X"™ from "Life Ambushes." He provides speaking, workshops, online programs, executive coaching, and business consulting to businesses around the world and group coaching through his "Get off the X Training and Overcome Army"™ programs.

Jason has appeared on numerous national news networks including Fox News, CBS, CNN, and CBN. He has appeared frequently on *Fox and Friends* and the *Huckabee* show. Jason has appeared in multiple documentaries including the History Channel's *Navy SEALs: America's Secret Warriors*.

ABOUT THE AUTHOR

To learn more about Jason Redman
or hire him for speaking opportunities, go to
www.jasonredman.com

To learn more about Jason Redman's coaching and
online programs, go to
www.getoffx.com